W0108064

THE
THUGS
OR
PHANSIGARS OF INDIA

THE
THUGS
OR
PHANSIGARS OF INDIA

COMPRISING A

HISTORY OF THE RISE AND PROGRESS

OF THAT

EXTRAORDINARY FRATERNITY OF ASSASSINS;

AND A

DESCRIPTION OF THE SYSTEM WHICH IT PURSUES, AND OF THE MEASURES WHICH HAVE BEEN ADOPTED BY THE SUPREME GOVERNMENT OF INDIA FOR ITS SUPPRESSION

VOLUME I

Compiled from Original and Authentic Documents published

By

CAPTAIN W. H. SLEEMAN

Published by

Gyan Publishing House
5, Ansari Road
Daryaganj, New Delhi-110002
Phone: 011-47034999, 9811692060
E-mail: books@gyanbooks.com

Distribution Network
gyanbooks.com
India, USA, Canada, UK, Australia, France

© Publisher

All rights reserved. No part of this work may be reproduced, stored, adapted, or transmitted in any form or by any means, electronic, mechanical, photocopying, micro-filming, recording or otherwise, or translated in any language, without the prior written permission of the copyright owner and the publisher.

ISBN : 978-81-212-9080-7 (Set)
978-81-212-9809-4 (HB)
First Published, 1839

2nd Impression 2023

Printed at: Gyan Press, Delhi.

The book is sold subject to the condition that it shall not, by way of trade or otherwise, be lent, resold, hired out, or otherwise circulated without the prior publisher's written consent.

THE THUGS OR PHANSIGARS OF INDIA (VOL-1)
Author: CAPTAIN W. H. SLEEMAN

THE

THUGS

OR

PHANSIGARS OF INDIA:

COMPRISING A

HISTORY OF THE RISE AND PROGRESS

OF THAT

EXTRAORDINARY FRATERNITY OF ASSASSINS;

AND A

DESCRIPTION OF THE SYSTEM WHICH IT PURSUES, AND OF THE
MEASURES WHICH HAVE BEEN ADOPTED BY THE SUPREME
GOVERNMENT OF INDIA FOR ITS SUPPRESSION.

Compiled from Original and Authentic Documents published

By CAPTAIN W. H. SLEEMAN,

SUPERINTENDENT OF THUG POLICE.

1839.

PREFACE.

THE history of the Thugs, comprised in the
following pages, has been chiefly compiled from a
volume published in Calcutta in 1836, entitled,
" Ramaseana, or a Vocabulary of the peculiar·
" Language used by the Thugs, with an Introduc-
" tion and Appendix, descriptive of the System
" pursued by that Fraternity, and of the Measures
".adopted by the Supreme Government of India
" for it suppression."
The author, Captain W. H. Sleeman of the
Indian military service, who has recently occupied
the station of Superintendent of the Thug Police,
has devoted but a few pages of his voluminous
work to the vocabulary referred to in the title.
The remainder of the work is composed of an
Introduction, comprising notices of the system of
the Thugs, and of the operations pursued by the
government for extirpating them; a series of conversations with Thug informers, containing full
and most extraordinary disclosures respecting their
superstitions and crimes; and an immense mass of
official papers relating to the apprehension of
various gangs of Thugs, their trials and executions.
*

From this repository of undigested materials, the compiler of the volume now offered to the public, has endeavoured to form a clear and succinct account of the Thugs, their peculiar superstitions, their methods of proceeding in robbing and murdering travellers, and the operations of the British government in India for the extirpation of this singular and unparalled system of assassination and plunder. To this he has added an Appendix, containing the vocabulary of their language, the disclosures made to Captain Sleeman by Thug informers, and a specimen of the trials of some of the criminals; which serves to exhibit the careful and impartial system pursued by the British authorities in bringing these atrocious criminals to justice.

The information contained in the following pages, will be found to exhibit a most extraordinary and interesting chapter in the history of human character. It brings to light the astounding fact, that for a period of two hundred years, there has existed in India a secret association of assassins, bound together by a peculiar system of superstition, and successfully pursuing robbery and murder as a regular means of subsistence; that this association was, or rather *is*, composed of many thousand persons; that by a process of early education and gradual training its members are brought to consider murder and robbery as no crimes, but rather as religious acts, well pleasing to their tutelary deity; and finally, that their measures have been so cunningly concerted, and carefully pursued, that until within a very recent period, not one in a hundred of them has ever been brought to answer to any human tribunal for his atrocious crimes. The reader will have the satisfaction, however, of learning, that the energetic measures now in operation for suppressing this abominable fraternity, afford a fair presumption that its existence will speedily terminate.

Aware that the principal value of the work depends upon the amount of authentic information which it comprises, the compiler has presented the several portions of it as nearly in the state in which each is furnished by the original writer, as was consistent with the clearness and brevity necessary to commend it to the notice of the general reader. The arrangement which he has adopted, is believed to be such as will afford the reader a satisfactory general view of the subject in the main body of the work; with the means of gratifying curiosity, as to its minuter details and ramifications, in the Appendix. To the inquirer into human character and the motives and springs of action which influence the conduct of men under extraordinary circumstances, the whole will form a most curious and interesting study.

CONTENTS.

CONTENTS. 11

HISTORY

THUGS OR PHANSIGARS.

[The first satisfactory general notice which we find of the Thugs, is contained in the following account from the pen of Doctor Richard C. Sherwood, Surgeon on the Establishment of Fort St. George. It was written in 1816; and refers to the Thugs as they were found at that time in the southern part of Hindoostan, under the name of Phansigars. The notes which illustrate it were written by Captain Sleeman, with all the advantages of his subsequent investigations, personal and historical, in 1816.]

WHILE Europeans have journeyed through the extensive territories subject to the Government of Fort St. George, with a degree of security no where surpassed, the path of the native traveller has been beset with perils little known or suspected, into which numbers annually falling, have mysteriously disappeared, the victims of villains as subtle, rapacious, and cruel, as any who are to be met with in the records of human depravity.

The Phansigars, or stranglers, are thus designated from the Hindustani word *phansi*, a noose. In the more northern parts of India, these mur-

2

derers are called *Thugs*, signifying deceivers : in
the Tamul language, they are called *Ari Tulucar*,
or Mussulman noosers : in Canarese, *Tanti Cal-
leru*, implying thieves, who use a wire or cat-gut
noose : and in Telagu, *Warlu Wahndlu*, or *Warlu
Vayshay Wahndloo*, meaning people who use the
noose.

There is no reason to believe that Europeans
were aware of the existence of such criminals as
Phansigars, until shortly after the conquest of Serin-
gapatan in 1799 ; when about a hundred were
apprehended in the vicinity of Bangalore. They
did not engage general attention ; nor would it
appear that they were suspected to belong to a
distinct class of hereditary murderers and plunder-
ers, settled in various parts of India, and alike
remarkable for the singularity of their practice, and
the extent of their depredations.   In the year 1807,
between Chittoor and Arcot, several Phansigars
were apprehended, belonging to a gang which had
just returned, laden with booty, from an expedition to Travancore, and information was then
obtained, which ultimately led to the developement
of the habits, artifices, and combinations of these
atrocious delinquents.

The Phansigars that infested the South of India
a few years ago, were settled in Mysore, on the
borders of that kingdom and the Carnatic, in the
Balaghat districts, ceded to the Company by the
Nizam in 1800, and they were particularly numerous in the Poliums of Chittoor.   The sequestered
part of the country, which comprehended these
Poliums, maintaining little intercourse with the
neighbouring districts, abounding in hills and fast-
nesses, and being immediately subject to several
Polygars, afforded the Phansigars a convenient

and secure retreat; and the protection of the Polygars was extended to them, in common with other classes of robbers, in consideration of a settled contribution, or, which was more frequent, of sharing in the fruits of their rapacity.

It was impossible that such criminals as Phansigars, living by systematic plans of depredation, could long remain in the same place in safety, unless their practices were encouraged or connived at by persons in authority. Hence, after the establishment of the Company's Government over the Carnatic, and the Districts ceded by the Nizam, and the consequent extinction of the power and influence of the Polygars, some of whom had succeeded in rendering themselves virtually independent of the former government, these murderers very generally changed their abodes, and frequently assumed other names.

While they lived under the protection of Polygars and other petty local authorities, and among people whose habits were in some respects analogous to their own, it was unnecessary to dissemble that they subsisted by depredation. They and their families lived peaceably with their neighbours, whom they never attempted to molest, and between whom there subsisted a reciprocation of interest in the purchase and disposal of the plunder which the Phansigars brought with them on returning from their expeditions. Afterwards, on the extension of the English government, it was usual for the Phansigars, while they continued their former practices, ostensibly to engage in the cultivation of land or some other occupation, to screen themselves from suspicion to which they must otherwise have been obnoxious.*

* They at all times engaged in the tillage of land even under

Phansigars never commit robbery unaccompanied by murder, their practice being first to strangle and then to rifle their victims. It is also a principle with them to allow no one to escape of a party however numerous, which they assail, that there may be no witnesses of their atrocities. The only admitted exception to this rule is in the instance of boys of very tender age, who are spared, adopted by the Phansigars, and, on attaining the requisite age, initiated into their horrible mysteries.*

A gang of Phansigars consists of from ten to fifty, or even a greater number of persons, a large majority of whom are Mussulmans; but Hindus, and particularly those of the Rajput tribe, are often associated with them.† Bramins, too, though rarely, are found in the gangs.‡ Emerging from their haunts, they sometimes perform long journeys, being absent from home many months, and prowl along the eastern and western coasts to Hyderabad and Cape Comorin. In general, however, they do

the Native Chiefs when they had settled habitations. They eithe sowed the lands or prepared them for the seed during the season they remained at home, and left the care of them to their old men, women and children while on their expeditions.   W. H. S.

* Girls of very tender age and high cast are also often spared, and when they grow up married to the sons of Thugs. Women too are often separated from the parties of travellers on some pretence or other and saved by most classes of Thugs.   W. H. S.

† The gangs have often consisted of two and three hundred, though on such occasions they commonly follow each other in small parties of ten or twenty, or operate on roads parallel to each other, and prepared to concentrate on any point when necessary.
                                                                W. H. S.

‡ Bramins, it is probable, do not assist in the actual perpetration of murder, but are employed to procure intelligence, in obtaining which their peculiar privileges afford them great facilities.
Bramins strangle just as often as others; and are strangled by them without distinction.   W. H. S.

not roam to such a distance, but make one or two excursions every year.* Their victims are almost exclusively travellers whom they fall in with on the road. Each gang has its sirdar or leader, who directs its movements. Of a numerous gang, some usually remain at home, while the rest are engaged in the work of pillage and murder. Those that are abroad are often divided into separate parties of ten or fifteen persons, who either follow each other at some distance, or, the parties taking different routes, they rendezvous at an appointed place in advance, measures being at the same time taken to secure a speedy junction of the gang, should this be requisite for the purpose of attacking several travellers at once. Different gangs sometimes act in concert, occasionally apprising one another of the approach of travellers whose destruction promises a rich booty.

Phansigars have the appearance of ordinary inoffensive travellers, and seldom assume any particular disguise. They indeed not unfrequently pretend to be traders, and there is reason to believe that they sometimes come from the Dukhun clothed in the garb of Bairagis. Formerly, when Phansigary was practised to a greater extent, and in a more daring manner than at present, the leader, especially if enriched by former spoliations, often travelled on horseback, with a tent, and passed for a person of consequence or a wealthy merchant,

---

* In the districts between the Ganges and Jumna, there were some associations of Thugs that seldom went far from home, and who made short and frequent expeditions. So the Jumaldehee Thugs of Oude and the neighbouring districts, so some of the Thug families in Bundelcund. Generally, however, the Thugs north of the Nurbudda, have been in the habit of making long expeditions, and remaining absent from six to eight months on each. W. H. S.

2 *

otherwise he appeared at first in a more humble character, and assumed in the course of his rapacious progress one of more importance, as he became possessed of horses and bullocks, which while they afforded him carriage for the plundered property, subserved the purpose of giving countenance and support to his feigned character.* -

Phansigars are accustomed to wait at Choultries on the high roads, or near to towns where travellers are wont to rest.   They arrive at such places and enter towns and villages in straggling parties of three or four persons, appearing to meet by accident and to have had no previous acquaintance. On such occasions, some of the gang are employed as emissaries to collect information, and especially to learn if any persons with property in their possession are about to undertake a journey.   They are often accompanied by children of ten years of age and upwards, who, while they perform menial offices, are initiated into the horrid practices of the Phansigars, and contribute to prevent suspicion of their real character.   Skilled in the arts of deception, they enter into conversation and insinuate themselves, by obsequious attentions, into the confidence of travellers of all descriptions, to learn from them whence they come, whither and for what purpose they are journeying, and of what property they are possessed ;—thus—

"—— under fair pretence of friendly ends,
And well placed words of glozing courtesy,
Baited with reasons not unplausible,
Wind them into the easy-hearted man;
And hug them into snares."

* They still continue to assume all kinds of disguises, and in every considerable gang there are some who feign to be men of high rank, as merchants or the public servants of some Native Government.

When the Phansigars determine, after obtaining such information as they deem requisite, to attack a traveller, they usually propose to him, under the specious plea of mutual safety, or for the sake of society, to travel together, or else they follow him at a little distance, and on arriving at a convenient place, and a fit opportunity presenting for effectuating their purpose, one of the gang suddenly puts a rope or sash round the neck of the unfortunate person, while others assist in depriving him of life.*

Two Phansigars are considered to be indispensable to effect the murder of one man, and commonly three are engaged. There is some variation in the manner in which the act is perpetrated, but the following is perhaps the most general. While travelling along, one of the Phansigars suddenly puts the cloth round the neck of the person they mean to kill, and retains hold of one end, while the other end is seized by an accomplice; the instrument crossed behind the neck is drawn tight, the two Phansigars pressing the head forwards; at the same time the third villain, in readiness behind the traveller, seizes his legs, and he is thrown forward upon the ground. In this situation he can make little resistance. The man holding the legs of the miserable sufferer, now kicks him in those parts of

They become acquainted with some officers of rank about Court whom they conciliate by handsome presents, who can serve them in time of need, and about whom they can always talk familiarly to travellers of rank whom they intend to kill.   W. H. S.

* If the traveller suspects one small party, he soon falls in with another, who seem to enter into his feelings of distrust. The first party is shaken off and the second destroys him. If there is only one party, or the travellers suspect and avoid the whole, two men are placed to watch their motions: and one follows them up, while the other informs the gang of their movements. W. H. S.

the body endowed with most sensibility, and he is quickly despatched.*

Antecedently to the perpetration of the murder, some of the gang are sent in advance, and some left in rear of the place, to keep watch and prevent intrusion by giving notice, on occasion, to those engaged in the act. Should any persons unexpectedly appear on the road, before the murdered body is buried, some artifice is practised to prevent discovery, such as covering the body with a cloth, while lamentations are made professedly on account of the sickness or death of one of their comrades; or one of the watchers falls down, apparently writhing with pain, in order to excite the pity of the intruding travellers and to detain them from the scene of murder.

Such are the perseverance and caution of the Phansigars, that a convenient opportunity not offering, they will sometimes travel in company with, or pursue persons whom they have devoted to destruction several days before they execute their intention. If circumstances favour them, they generally commit murder in a jungle or in an unfrequently part of the country, and near to a sandy place or dry water-course.† A hole three or four

---

* Some Thugs pride themselves upon being able to strangle a man single-handed; and, in speaking of an absent or deceased Thug, mention this as the highest compliment they could pay him. A man who has been able unassisted to pull a man from his horse and strangle him will confer a distinction upon his family for several generations. Such a man was Bukshee, whose head was preserved by Doctor Spry, and I have heard of a few others.
W. H. S. .

† Particular tracts were chosen in every part of India where they could murder their victims with the greatest convenience and security. Much frequented roads passing through extensive jungles, where the ground was soft for the grave, or the jungle thick to cover them, and the local authorities took no notice of the bodies.

feet in depth, in such a spot, is dug with facility, in which the body being placed, with the face downwards, it is shockingly mangled. Deep and continued gashes are often made in it in both sides, from the shoulders to the hands and to the feet, which lay open the abdomen and divide the tendon at the heel. Wounds are also made between the ribs into the chest, and sometimes if the hole be short, the knees are disjointed, and the legs turned back upon the body. The hole is then filled with earth. The body is thus cut and disfigured to expedite its dissolution, as well as to prevent its inflation, which, by raising or causing fissures in the superincumbent sand might attract jackals, and lead to the exposure of the corpse. When the amount of the property is less than they expected to find, the villains sometimes give vent to their disappointment in wanton indignities on the dead body.

If, when a murder is perpetrated, a convenient place for interring the body be not near, or if the Phansigars be apprehensive of discovery, it is either tied in a sack and carried to some spot, where it is not likely to be found, or it is put into a well;* or which is frequently practised, a shallow hole is dug, in which the corpse is buried, till a fit place for interring it can be discovered, when it is

The Thugs speak of such places with affection and enthusiasm, as other men would of the most delightful scenes of their early life. The most noted were among the Thugs of Hindostan. W. H. S.

* In Oude where the fields are almost all irrigated from wells, the bodies are generally thrown into them, and when the Cultivators discovered them, they hardly ever thought it worth while to ask how they got there, so accustomed were they to find them. In Bengal and Behar where the most frequented roads pass along, or frequently across rivers, the bodies are commonly thrown into them. W. H. S.

removed and cut in the manner already mentioned. If the traveller had a dog, it is also killed, lest the faithful animal should cause the discovery of the body of his murdered master. The office of mangling the dead body is usually assigned to a particular person of the gang. The Phansigars are always provided with knives and pick axes, which they conceal from observation.

From the foregoing account it will be obvious, that the system of the Phansigars is but too well adapted for concealment. The precautions they take, the artifices they practise, the mode of destroying their victims, calculated at once to preclude almost the possibility of rescue or escape—of witnesses of the deed—of noise or cries for help—of effusion of blood—and, in general, of all traces of murder :—these circumstances conspire to throw a veil of darkness over their atrocities.*

I now proceed to notice various particulars, more fully illustrating the practices, habits, and character of these criminals.

It is not improbable that formerly a long string, with a running noose, might have been used by Phansigars for seizing travellers, and that they robbed on horseback. But be this as it may, a noose is now, I believe, never thrown by them from a distance, in this part of India. They sometimes use a short rope, with a loop at one end, but a turban or a dothi (a long narrow cloth, or sash worn about the waist,) are more commonly employed; these serve the purpose as effectually as a regularly prepared noose, with this advantage that they do not tend to excite suspicion. When such a cloth

---

* If a Thug has been wounded in strangling a traveller, they pretend to have been attacked by robbers, and take him to the nearest station without any fear of discovery.   W. H. S.

is used, it is, previously to applying it, doubled to the length of two or two and a half feet, and a knot is formed at the double extremity, and about eighteen inches from it a slip knot is tied. In regulating the distance of the two knots, so that the intervening space when tightly twisted, may be adapted to embrace the neck, the Phansigar who prepares the instrument ties it upon his own knee. The two knots give the Phansigars a firm hold of the cloth, and prevent its slipping through their. hands in the act of applying it. After the person they attack has been brought to the ground, in the manner already described, the slip knot is loosed by the Phansigar who has hold of that part of the cloth, and he makes another fold of it round the neck, upon which, placing his foot, he draws the cloth tight, in a manner similar to that (to use the expression of my Phansigar informer) " of packing a bundle of straw."

Sometimes the Phansigars have not time to observe all the precautions I have mentioned in cutting and interring a body; apprehensions for their own safety inducing them to leave it slightly buried. Sometimes, also, when a murder is perpetrated in a part of the country which exposes them to the risk of observation, they put up a screen, or the wall for a tent, and bury the body within the inclosure, pretending if inquiries are made, that their women are within the screen. On such occasions, these obdurate wretches do not hesitate to dress and eat their food on the very spot where their victim is inhumed.

If, which scarcely ever happens, a traveller escape from the persons attempting to strangle him, he incurs the hazard of being dispatched by

one of the parties on watch.* Should he finally
escape, or should any other circumstance occur to
excite alarm or apprehensions of being seised, the
gang immediately disperses, having previously
agreed to re-assemble at an appointed time, at some
distant place.

Travellers resting in the same Choultry with
Phansigars are sometimes destroyed in the night,
and their bodies conveyed to a distance and buried.
On these occasions, a person is not always murdered when asleep; as, while he is in a recumbent
posture, the Phansigars find a difficulty in applying
the cloth. The usual practice is first to awaken
him suddenly with an alarm of a snake or a scor-
pion, and then to strangle him.†

In attacking a traveller on horseback, the Phansigars range themselves in the following manner.
One of the gang goes in front of the horse, and
another has his station in the rear : a third, walking
by the side of the traveller, keeps him engaged in
conversation till, finding that he is off his guard, he
suddenly seizes the traveller by the arm and drags
him to the ground, the horse at the same time
being seized by the foremost villain. The miserable sufferer is then strangled in the usual manner.

Against Phansigars it must be obvious, that arms
and the ordinary precautions taken against robbers,
are unavailing. When a person is armed with a
dagger, it is usual for one of the villains to secure
his hands. It sometimes happens, that a party of
travellers, consisting of several persons, and pos-

* These men have swords, and will endeavour to cut down any
man who escapes from the stranglers.   W. H. S.

† Travellers have been very often buried in the rooms in which
they have been strangled in Suraes, and large towns. If the house
be occupied, the occupants are in leage with the Thugs, of course.
                                                        W. H. S.

sessed of valuable effects, are, while journeying in imaginary security, suddenly cut off; and the lifeless and despoiled bodies being removed and interred, not a vestige of them appears.* Instances are said to have occurred, of twelve and fourteen persons being simultaneously destroyed. But such occurrences must be rare; and, in general, the property taken is not considerable. Such, indeed, are the cruelty and cupidity of these detestable wretches, that, on the presumption of every traveller possessing concealed treasure, or some property, however trifling, even indigence affords not its wonted security.

Formerly, if good horses, shawls, or other valuable articles, were among the booty, they were commonly reserved for the Polygar, in payment of protection. A portion of the plunder was usually appropriated to defraying the expenses of religious ceremonies; and sometimes, a part was also allotted for the benefit of widows and families of deceased members of the gang. The residue of the booty, being divided into several parts, was usually shared as follows:—to the leader two shares; to the men actually concerned in perpetrating the murder, and to the person who cut the dead body, each one share and a half, and to the remainder of the gang

* Near Sadras, about ten years ago, three *golah* peons were killed, having on them money in different coins, to the amount of 16,000 rupees. In 1805, five persons were killed in Coimbatoor, and cash to the amount of 2,500 pagodas, the property of the Collector of the district, was taken. In the same year, two respectable natives, proceeding on horseback from Madras to the Malabar coast, with five attendants, were all killed. In 1807, five persons, besides two others who had joined them on the road, were killed near Bangalore, and robbed of property to the amount of 1,000 pagodas, belonging to an officer of engineers. And in 1815, three persons were killed in the district of Masulipatam; and 2,500 rupees taken.

each one share. The plunder was almost always carried home by the Phansigars and sold greatly below its value. It was never disposed of near to the place where the person to whom it belonged was murdered, nor where it was likely to be recognized, of which the Phansigars were enabled-to judge by the information imparted to them by the credulous sufferers.*

The frequent association of the most abject superstition, with the deepest guilt, has been often noticed. The justness of the observation is exemplified in the conduct of most, perhaps of all classes of Indian delinquents, and remarkably so in that of the Phansigars. Their system, indeed, seems to be founded on the basis of superstition. They pay the most servile regard to omens; and they never leave their abodes to go on an expedition, without a previous persuasion, derived from modes of divination in use among them, that it will be attended with success. Though the Phansigars are almost all Mussulmans, they have nevertheless universally adopted, on certain occasions, the idolatrous worship of Hindu deities. *Cali* or *Marriatta* (the goddess of small pox of the Carnatic) is regarded as their tutelary deity, and is the object of their adoration. She is usually invoked by them under the name of *Javi* or *Ayi* and of *Tuljapuri.*† Before

---

* The property was generally disposed of near the place where the murders were perpetrated when the travellers were from distant parts; but at villages off the main road or in advance of the place, and not at places where the travellers had rested or been seen.   W. H. S.

† Colonel Colin Mackenzie, so well known for his successful researches into Indian history and antiquities, observes in a letter to me, " that it was the custom of many of the ancient heads of families, that have raised themselves by depredation to rank and power, to conciliate *Cali*; hence the sacrifices of human kind, of offerings of horses and ultimately of sheep by the Rajahs of Mysore,

an expedition is determined on, an entertainment is given, when the ceremony of sacrificing a sheep to *Jyu* is performed; and though perhaps not always, yet it would seem generally in the following manner. A silver or brazen image of the goddess, with certain paraphernalia pertaining to her; and sometimes also, one of *Ganesa*; and the images of a lizard and a snake, reptiles from which presages are drawn; together with the implements of Phansigari, as a noose, knife, and pick-axe, being placed together, flowers are scattered over them, and offerings of fruit, cakes, spirits, &c. are made; oderiferous powders are burned, and prayers are offered for success. The head of the sheep being cut off, it is placed, with a burning lamp upon it and the right forefoot in the mouth, before the image of *Jayi*, and the goddess is entreated to reveal to them, whether she approves of the expedition they are meditating. Her consent is supposed to be declared, should certain tremulous or convulsive movements be observed, during the invocation, in the mouth and nostrils, while some fluid is poured upon those parts. But the absence of those agitations is considered as indicating the disapprobation of the goddess, and the expedition is postponed.

and now the commutation of cocoanuts at the hill of Mysore, which derives its name from *Mahes Asura Mardana*, another name for *Cali*.

"At Chitteldroog also, the ancient Polygars worshipped and sacrificed to *Cali*, and even still at *Taljupur* on the western ghauts, 300 miles west of Hydrabed, on the road to Poonah. I was there in March 1797. It is a celebrated temple of *Cali*, where the poojah is performed by a low tribe, and not by bramins, who abhor these rites. It is even so much suspected that infamous rites and human victims were offered there, that my head bramin (the late valued *Boriar*,) horror-struck by the accounts he received, urged my departure from *Taljapur*, and was not easy till we got away.

About ten or twenty days afterwards, the ceremony is repeated; and if auspicious inferences be drawn from it, the Phansigars prepare to depart. But before they determine towards what quarter to proceed, some persons of the gang are sent on the high road, in the direction they wish to take, to observe the flight of crows and other birds, and to listen to the chirping of lizards. Should success be betokened, the same path is taken. If the signs be adverse, the sirdar sends some of the gang to make observations on another road, or at a place where two roads meet, and these votaries of superstition proceed in that direction, which promises, as they infer, the best success.

In the course of their progress, they observe the same scrupulous regard to omens. Emboldened by favourable ones, they are greatly discouraged by those of an opposite tendency. If they have not proceeded far from home, when unlucky signs are descried, they regard them as premonitions to return : under other circumstances they either perform certain ceremonies, or they halt for a few days, till the malignant influence, denoted by them, is supposed to be past, or else they bend their course in a different direction. To the intervention of bad omens, a traveller, over whom destruction was impending, is sometimes indebted for his safety.*

---

* It would be tedious to enumerate all the omens by which they allow themselves to be influenced in their proceedings. I shall briefly mention a few of both kinds, prosperous and adverse.

The following are favourable signs : A lizard chirping, and a crow making a noise on a living tree on the left side. A tiger appearing is deemed rather a good sign. The noise of a partridge on the right side, denotes that they will meet with good booty on the very spot, and they, therefore, are accustomed to make a halt.

These betoken misfortune. A hare or a snake crossing the

On returning also from a successful expedition, ceremonies are performed to *Jayi*.

The Phansigars keep the Hindu festivals of the *Dipivali* and the *Desserah*, which they celebrate in a manner similar to that observed among Hindus.

A tradition is current among Phansigars, that about the period of the commencement of the *Cali Yug, Mariatta* co-operated with them so far, as to relieve them of the trouble of interring the dead bodies, by devouring them herself. On one occasion, after destroying a traveller, the body was, as usual, left unburied; and a novice unguardedly looking behind him, saw the goddess in the act of feasting upon it, half of it hanging out of her mouth. She, upon this, declared that she would no longer devour those whom the Phansigars slaughtered; but she condescended to present them with one of her teeth for a pickaxe, a rib for a knife, and the hem of her lower garment for a noose, and ordered them, for the future, to cut and bury the bodies of those whom they destroyed.

White and yellow being considered the favourite colours of their patroness, and those in which she is arrayed; the cloths for strangling are of one or other of these, to the exclusion, I believe, of all other colours.

Ridiculous as their superstitions must appear, they are not devoid of effect. They serve the important purposes of cementing the union of the gang; of kindling courage and confidence; and, by an appeal to religious texts deemed infallible, of

road before them. A crow sitting and making a noise on a rock or a dead tree. An ass braying while sitting. An owl screeching. The noise of a single jackal. If a dog should carry off the head of a sheep which they have sacrificed, they consider it to betoken that they will get no booty for many years.

3*

imparting to their atrocities the semblance of divine sanction.

To the ascendancy of the same superstitious feeling is also to be ascribed the curious circumstance that Phansigars are accustomed to refrain from murdering females, and persons of the Camala cast; which includes gold, iron, and brass-smiths, carpenters and stone-cutters, washermen, pot-makers, pariahs, chucklers, lepers; the blind and mutilated, a man driving a cow or a female goat, are also spared. These persons appear to be regarded either as the descendants or servants of *Jayi*, as her constant worshippers; or as having claims to the especial protection of the goddess, and are for these reasons exempted from slaughter.

When this rule is respected, any one of these persons, travelling with others of different castes, proves a safeguard to the whole party; the same principle which prompts the Phansigars to destroy every individual of a party, forbidding them to kill any unless the whole.

Many Phansigars, who have become informers, have declared that they never knew any of the above-mentioned persons to have been destroyed, and conceived that no pecuniary temptation could be sufficiently powerful to occasion a violation of the rule. Others have stated that they had heard of a gang of Phansigars who, having murdered a woman, never afterwards prospered, and were at length destroyed. Notwithstanding the reasons for acquiescing generally in the truth of the statement, that women, and men of particular castes, are spared, the following occurrences, in the latter of which not fewer than nine persons disappeared, and who were almost beyond doubt murdered by Phansigars, shew that their religious scruples on this point are, when the temptation is great, at least sometimes overcome.

In the latter end of 1800, Mohamed Rous, the Subadar who commanded the escort of the Resident of Mysore, being ordered to join the force then forming against the Southern Polygars, sent some of his family, among whom were two, if not three, women, to Madras. They were never heard of until June 1801, when a man was seized at Bangalore, having in his possession a bullock which was recognized to have belonged to Mahomed Rous. This man was a Phansigar, and gave a clear account of the murder, by a gang to which he belonged, of the Subadar's family.

The wife of Kistna Row, in company with his nephew, and attended by a bramin cook, two female servants, two private peons, and two coolies, set out from Poonah with four horses to join Kistna Row, then at Nagpur. They had nearly completed their journey, having arrived at a village about fifteen miles from the place of their destination, and sent to apprize Kistna Row of their approach. Two persons were sent by him to conduct the party to Nagpur; but subsequently to the departure of the travellers from the village above-mentioned no intelligence could be obtained—no traces whatever could be discovered of them; and though about four years have since elapsed, all inquiries have been fruitless.*

---

* I have stated that nine persons were cut off on this occasion, though there is some reason to believe that the party consisted of even a greater number.

Kistna Row had been formerly employed in the confidential situation of Shirishtedar under Colonel Read, when this gentleman held the Collectorship of the Territories ceded by Tippoo, on the conclusion of the war of 1793. He afterwards served under Colonel Close, at the Residency at Poonah, where he is still employed by the British Government.

The utility to such criminals as Phansigars of
signs, and of words and phrases not understood by
others, as channels of communication, must be
obvious. It is accordingly found that several such
are employed by them. Some of those in more
frequent use I shall mention; and the catalogue
might have been easily extended.

Drawing the back of the hand along the chin,
from the throat outwards, implies that caution
is requisite—that some stranger is approaching.
Putting the open hand over the mouth and drawing
it gently down implies that there is no longer cause
for alarm. If an advanced party of Phansigars
overtake any traveller whom they design to destroy, but have need of more assistance, they make
certain marks on the roads, by which those of the
gang who follow understand that they are required
to hasten forwards. A party in advance also
leaves certain marks where a road branches off, as
intimations to those who follow of the route their
comrades have taken.

The following list comprehends several slang
terms and phrases in use among them. This language they denominate *Pheraseri-ci-bat;* or as the
term may be rendered, the language of dispatch or
emergency:

Yetu,	one.	Sitcale,	pagoda.
Bitri,	two.	Burce,	rupee.
Sancod,	three.	Chilta,	fanam.
Wodli,	four.	Sitac,	gold.
Panchuru,	five.	Cawridga,	silver.
Serlu and Cheru,	six.	Curp,	a horse.
Sathuni,	seven.	Curpani,	a mare.
Desur,	ten.	Newala,	sheep.
Mahi,	one hundred.	Samcani,	a hare.
Hacade,	one thousand.	Moz (per)	bullock.
Doacade,	two thousand.	Agasi,	turban.
Desacade,	ten thousand.	Raclan (per)	jackal.

Comuda (h) ....coek.
Comudi (h)..............hen.
Sendri, ...coral.
Pandur-phali,...........pearl.
Shaick-ji, or Ma- } Mussulman
  homed Khan, { stranger.
Bhitu,.............Hindu do.
Cantger (per)........watcher.
Chaicari, ...intelligencer.
Worawal,.. { Persons appoint-
            { ed to seize horse-
            { men.
Mahi,..............pickaxe.
Cathmi, ... { knife for cutting
            { the dead body.

Rumal, { handker-
       { chief worn   } *Various articles used for strang-*
       { as a turban. } *ling.*
Cancha (h).. } sash
Dhoti (tel) .. } sash
Newar (h).....tape
Nar Muctem,......
Sir-ghant.........chief knot.
Der-ghant......1½ or slip knot.
Man, . { a convenient place for
       { murdering.
Cont, . { name of an enter-
        { tainment given by
        { Phansigars to their
        { friends.

	Literally.	*Phansigar Accep-tation.*
Nyamet,..........	A delicacy,........	A rich man.
Lacra, ...	A stick, ...	A man of no pro-perty.
Phankana, ...	....	Ditto.
Dhol, ...	A barber's drum,...	An old man.
Man Jharcerdo,....	Sweep the place,...	See that no person is near.
Kantna pantelao,...	Bring firewood,....	Take your allotted posts.
Pan ka rumal nica-lo, ...	Take out the hand-kerchief with the beetle,..........	Get out the doti, &c.
Pan Khao,........	Eat beetle,........	Despatch him.

Ronacero, ... Implies a slight burial, with the face downwards, the body whole and covered only with sufficient earth to conceal it.

Kedbi Gidbi, Dekho, Look after the straw, ... Look after the corpse, that is, the Phansigars proceed to a village after the slight burial, and send out the appointed persons to bury the body properly, keeping watch that no person is looking.

Kedba bahir pariya. The straw is come out,....... Jackals have taken out the corpse, you must not go that way.

Bhavani Puter, Descen- ⎫
dants of Bhowáni, ... ⎬   Phansigars?
Bhavani Putur, Town of ⎭
Bhowani Puter, ...

Used interrogatively to ascertain without the risk of exposing themselves, whether persons whom they meet on their journeys, and whom they suspect to be of the same fraternity, are so or not. When caution is particularly requisite, the question is put in the latter and less suspicious shape. The first syllable *put*, ascertains the point of their connexion with *Bhavani*, whilst from the termination *ur*, which signifies a town or village, they would appear to a stranger to be inquiring only about some particular place.

Phansigars bring up all their male children to the profession, unless bodily defects prevent them from following it. The method observed in initiating a boy is very gradual. At the age of ten or twelve years, he is first permitted to accompany a party of Phansigars. One of the gang, generally a near relation, becomes his *ustad* or tutor, whom the child is taught to regard with great respect, and whom he usually serves in a menial capacity, carrying a bundle, and dressing food for him. Frequently the father acts as the preceptor to his son. In the event of being questioned by travellers whom he may meet, the boy is enjoined to give no information further than that they are proceeding from some one place to another. He is instructed to consider his interest as opposed to that of society in general, and to deprive a human being of life is represented as an act merely analogous and equivalent to that of killing a fowl or a sheep. At first, while a murder is committing, the boy is sent to some distance from the scene, along with one of the watchers: then allowed to see only the dead body: afterwards more and more of the secret is imparted to him—and at length, the whole is disclosed. In the mean time a share of the booty is usually assigned to him. He is allowed afterwards to assist in matters of minor importance, while the murder is perpetrating: but it is not until he has attained the age of 18, 20, or 22 years, according to the bodily strength he may have acquired, and the prudence and resolution he may have evinced; that he is deemed capable of applying the *Dhouti*, nor is he allowed to do so, until he has been formally presented with one by his *ustad*. . For this purpose a fortunate day being fixed upon, and the time of the *Desserah* is deemed particularly auspicious, the preceptor takes his pupil apart and presents him with a *Dhouti*, which he tells him to use in the name of *Jayi;* he observes to him that on it he is to rely for the means of subsistence, and he exhorts him to be discreet and courageous. On the conclusion of this ceremony his education is considered to be complete, he is deemed qualified to act as a Phansigar, and he applies the noose on the next occasion that offers.

After his initiation, a Phansigar continues to treat his preceptor with great respect. He occasionally makes him presents, and assists him in his old age; and, on meeting him after a long absence, he touches his feet in token of reverence.

Such is the effect of the course of education I have described, strengthened by habit, that Phansigars become strongly attached to their detestable occupation. They rarely, if ever abandon it.*

* Three are known to have engaged in the serviee of the company as Sepoys. When elosely pursued, Thugs often enter the regiments of Native Chiefs, or engage in some other serviee till the

Some, narrowly escaping the merited vengeance of the law, and released from prison under security, could not refrain from resuming their old employment; and those who, bending under the weight of years and infirmities, are no longer able to bear an active or principal part, continue to aid the cause by keeping watch, procuring intelligence, or dressing the food of their younger confederates.

The bonds of social union among Phansigars are drawn still closer by intermarriages. Though not of frequent occurrence, instances are not wanting in which they have married into families deemed honest and respectable. The women are not ignorant of the proceedings of their husbands. Persons of mature age are very rarely admitted into the fraternity, and when this has been done, it was only after long and intimate intercourse had enabled the Phansigars fully to appreciate the character of their confederates.*

To the influence of personal character are Phansigars usually indebted for becoming the heads of gangs. Like others, who follow lawless and abandoned courses, the Phansigars are profligate and improvident, and addicted to the use of *bang*, so that the wealth they may acquire, even though considerable, is soon wasted.

Whether any Phansigar were ever capitally

danger is over. A great many of the most noted Thugs now in India, are in Seindheea's Regiments, at Gwalior, and in those of Oudepore, Joudpore, Jypore, &c., and it is almost impossible to get them, as they always make friends of the Commandants by their presents and their manners. Some are in the Baroda Rajah's service, others were in the King of Oude's service, but that is not now a safe one for them. W. H. S.

* North of the Nurbudda, the Thugs had for many years been in the habit of admitting into their gangs men of all ages and all casts. W. H. S.

punished by the Nabobs of the Carnatic, I know not. One gang, settled in the Polium of Chargal, near the Paidnaigdrug Pass, between the upper and lower Carnatic, was apprehended about 17 years ago, and fined to the amount of 5,000 rupees by the Subahdar of the province; a mode of punishment so far from being justifiable, that it could hardly have been imposed except from sordid motives: nor could it fail to give new impulse to the activity of the Phansigars, and to render them more than ever rapacious and secret in their barbarous practices.*

Hyder Alli proceeded against these criminals in a very summary manner. and destroyed several of them. In the reign of Tippoo, some were sentenced to hard labour, and others suffered mutilation of the limbs. While Purniah was Dewan of Mysore, during the minority of the present Rajah, highway robbery being frequent, was made capital, and several Phansigars were executed.

It must be obvious that no estimate, except what is extremely vague and unsatisfactory, can be formed of the number of persons that have annually fallen victims to Phansigars in the south of India. The number has varied greatly at different periods. There is reason to believe, that from the time of the conquest of Mysore in 1799 to 1807 and 1808 the practice of Phansigari, in this part of India, had reached its acme, and that hundreds of persons were annually destroyed.† The great political

* Native Hindoo Princes, hardly ever punished these people, unless they had by some accident murdered some priest or public officer of the Court, in whom they feel particularly interested. While their grief or resentment lasted, they were seized and punished, but no longer. W. H. S.

† In one of his reports, the magistrate of Chittur observes—" I believe that some of the Phansigars have been concerned in above

changes, which marked the commencement of that period, and the introduction of a new system of government in Mysore, the ceded districts and the Carnatic, though infinitely preferable to the former, yet was it in many respects less zealous and vigilant, and afforded facilities of communication before unknown, between distant countries, of which the Phansigars and other criminals availed themselves to overspread the country: and it may be conjectured that many persons deprived by the declension of the Mohammedan power of their wonted resources, were tempted to resort to criminal courses to obtain a subsistence.

The foregoing description of the Phansigars is meant to be more particularly applicable to those gangs that were settled in the northern parts of the Carnatic and in the ceded districts, antecedently to the year 1808. Since that time, they have become well known to the English Courts of Justice, and their habits have undergone some changes. Many have left the Company's territories, and fled to those of the Nizam and of the Mahrattas. But though the number of them is greatly diminished, Phansigars still infest the dominions of the Company. The gangs indeed, consist of fewer persons than formerly; their plans are less systematic;

two hundred murders; nor will this estimate appear extravagant, if it be remembered, that murder was their profession, frequently their only means of gaining a subsistence: every man of fifty years of age, has probably been actively engaged during twenty-five years of his life in murder, and on the most moderate computation, it may be reckoned, that he has made one excursion a year, and met each time with ten victims."

Yet Francis Bartolomeo says, in a note page 69—" During a residence of 13 or 14 years in India, I never heard of any traveller being robbed or murdered on the highway."—*Travels in India*, *translated by Forster*.

their range is less ample ; they roam the country more secretly; more frequently changing their names and places of abode; and adopting other precautionary measures to screen themselves from justice. Unfortunately few of the numerous Phansigars that have at different times been apprehended could be convicted in accordance with the evidence required by the Mohammedan criminal law ; which admitting not the testimony of accomplices, and rarely the sufficiency of strong circumstantial evidence; unless confirmed by the confession of the culprits, their adherence to protestations of innocence has alone, but too frequently, exempted them from punishment. Those that have been tried and released becoming greater adepts in deceit, have, together with their old propensities, carried with them a knowledge of the form of trial, and of the nature of the evidence requisite to their conviction.

The habits and proceedings of the Phansigars, it is reasonable to conclude, have been modified and varied by different circumstances and events of a local or political nature in the several states infested by them, in some places approximating more than in others to the foregoing description. There is every reason to believe that in the Deccan, and more particularly in the territories of the Nizam, Phansigars are very numerous. They will be naturally encouraged to settle in greater numbers, and to carry on their practises with less caution and secresy, in a country a prey to anarchy or invasion, where the administration is feeble or corrupt, or where crimes are constantly committed with impunity. It is also not unreasonable to suppose, that they may occasionally act in concert with other classes of delinquents, and that their proceedings may sometimes be of a mixed nature,

partaking of the peculiarities of those with whom
they may be in league. In those countries, too,
where Phansigari has been long practised, it may
be presumed, that the ordinary artifices will at
length become known, and as the success of those
murderers must chiefly depend on the ignorance of
travellers of their devices, they will perhaps find it
necessary to resort to novel and unsuspected strat-
gems.*

I have heard of no instance in which a European
was murdered by Phansigars. The manner in
which they are accustomed to travel in India, is
perhaps sufficient to exempt them from danger ;
added to which, apprehension of the consequences
of strict inquiry and search, should an European
be missing, may be supposed to intimidate the
Phansigars, at least in the dominions of the company. Similar reasons influence them in sparing
coolies and parties charged with the property of
English gentlemen, combined with the consideration that while such articles would generally be
useless to the Phansigars, they would find difficulty
in disposing of them, and might incur imminent
danger of detection in the attempt.

That the disappearance of such numbers of
natives should have excited so little interest and
inquiry as not to have led to a general knowledge
of those combinations of criminals will naturally
appear extraordinary. Such ignorance, certainly,
could not have prevailed in England, where the

* There are a class of Byragee and Gosaen Thugs, who travel
about the country as religious mendicants, and rob and murder
occasionally. They pretend to alchemy, and getting the silver of
the credulous under a promise of converting it into gold, they make
off with it. They are well known to the Thugs, and often join
them in their murders, when they meet on the roads.

W. H. S. .

absence, if unaccounted for, of even a single person, seldom fails to produce suspicion, with consecutive investigation and discovery. In India the case is far otherwise: and such on event, unless occurring to a person of some consequence, would scarcely be known beyond the precincts of the place of residence or the village of the unfortunate sufferer. Many that fall victims to the Phansigars are the subjects of other and distant states, many have no settled abodes. It must also be remembered that Phansigars refrain from murdering the inhabitants of towns and villages near to which they are halting; neither are they accustomed to murder near to their own habitations, circumstances which not only prevent suspicion attaching to them as the murderers, and to the local authority as protecting and sharing the booty with them, but tend to throw it upon others, who reside near to the spot whither a traveller may have been traced, and where he was last seen. Besides a person setting out on a journey is often unable to fix any period for his return; and though he should not revisit his home, at the expected time, his delay will, for a while, excite little alarm, in the minds of his friends. He is supposed to be unexpectedly detained—to be ill—to have met with some ordinary accident—to have deserted his family—to have died. Should suspicion arise that he has been murdered, the act is attributed to ordinary highway robbers, and it is but seldom that minute inquiries can be instituted by his bereaved relatives. But supposing that this is done, and the progress of the missing traveller traced to a particular place and not beyond it, still suspicion would be apt to attach to any, rather than to a few apparently inoffensive travellers,

4*

journeying either for the purpose of traffic, as is imagined; or, as is often pretended, to see their relations, or to be present at some marriage, and who, if ever noticed, have perhaps been long since forgotten. If notwithstanding all these improbabilities, suspicion should fall upon the actual perpetrators, where could they be found?*

Thus with respect to Sepoys, who having obtained leave of absence, never rejoined their corps, the conclusion generally formed has been, that they had deserted,—when, in various instances, they had fallen sacrifices to the wiles of the Phansigars. The same observation is particularly applicable to golah peons, charged with the conveyance of money and valuables; many of whom having disappeared, no doubt was entertained that they had absconded, and appropriated the property to their own use. Even the apprehension, which an indistinct idea of danger tends to create in the minds of these and other travellers would render them only more liable to fall into the snare. Less persuasion would be requisite to induce them to join a party of Phansigars, prompted by the belief that they were thus providing, in the most effectual manner, for their own safety.

What constitutes the most odious feature in the character of these murderers is, that prodigal as they are of human life, they can rarely claim the benefit of even the palliating circumstance of strong pecuniary temptation. They are equally strangers to compassion and remorse—they are never re-

* To whom were the friends of the murdered to complain? it was equally unavailing to complain to the authorities of the district in which they were supposed to be murdered—that in which the suspected murderers resided, and that in which they themselves resided; and they had no others to complain to.

strained from the commission of crimes by com-
miseration for the unfortunate traveller—and they
are exempted from the compunctive visitings of
conscience, which usually follow, sooner or later,
the steps of guilt. " Phansigari," they observe
with cold indifference, blended with a degree of
surprise, when questioned on this subject, " is their
business," which, with reference to the tenets of
fatalism, they conceive themselves to have been
pre-ordained to follow. By an application of the
same doctrine, they have compared themselves,
not inaptly, to tigers, maintaining that as these
ferocious beasts are impelled by irresistible necessity, and fulfil the designs of nature in preying on
other animals, so the appropriate victims of the
Phansigars are men, and that the destiny of those
whom they kill " was written on their foreheads."*

This state of moral insensibility and debasement
is calculated to give birth to pity, while it aggra-
vates the horror with which we contemplate their
atrocities. It ought not to be forgotten that, unlike
many who adopt criminal courses, the Phansigars
had not previously to divest themselves of upright
principles, to oppose their practice to their feelings ;
but, that, on the contrary, having been trained
up from their childhood to the profession, they
acquired habits unfitting them for honest and indus-
trious exertion : that a detestable superstition lent
its sanctions to their enormities : and that they did
but obey the instructions, and imitate the examples
of their fathers.

* A Thug will never kill a tiger, and believes that no man who
has violated this rule ever survived long. They believe that no
tiger will ever kill a Thug, unless he has secreted some booty, or
cheated some of the gang out of their just share. A mere tyro or
understrapper, they think a tiger may kill, provided he be not of
good Thug descent. W. H. S.

The Thugs* in the more northern parts of India
may be divided into three classes. The first consists chiefly of Mahomedans who originally resided
under the protection of Zemindars of large estates,
as Hura Sing, Dia Ram, &c., and in the district of
Etawab, including also a few stranglers at other
villages.† The second class is composed of Hindus,
who are for the most part of the Lodeh caste, and
is much more numerous than the former.‡ They
resided in great numbers in their eastern part of
Etawah, and the adjoining district of Cawnpore,
until alarmed by the active exertions of the magistrates by whom many were apprehended.§ These
Thugs had long escaped suspicion by engaging in
tillage, and by always carrying on their depredations at a distance from home. The third class is
more considerable in respect to number, and extends
over a larger tract of country than either of the
foregoing classes. It consists of a desperate association of all castes, which grew up in the Pergunnahs
of Sindouse and Purhara, and the neighbouring
villages in the Mahratta territories.‖ They travel
in large bodies, and are more bold and adventurous

* The term Thug is not unknown in the South of India, but is
not applied to the Phansigars, but to a class of delinquents to whom
it seems more appropriate, viz. to cheats and swindlers, who often
appearing as pearl and coral sellers, practise various fraudulent
arts, particularly in substituting bad coins for good, which they
receive under pretence of giving or taking change.
    † These are the Sindouse men, and those of the adjoining Pur-
guna of Sursae.   W. H. S.
    ‡ These were the Behareepore, Tirwa and Oureya men, of the
districts of Cawnpore, and Furruckabad, and Belha. W. H. S.
    § Messrs. Stockwell, Halhed, Perry, Wright, and others.
                                                   W. H. S.
    ‖ These were the Sindouse and Sursae men, the same as first
named. The Sindouse villages were held by the Kuchwaha Rajpoots, and for that reason called Kuchwahadhar. The Sursae
villages were held by Purheear Rajpoots, and therefore called

than the Thugs in the Company's provinces. Their predatory excursions are chiefly confined to the country that lies to the eastward and southward of Gwalior, and to the province of Bundelcund.

Thevenot, in the following passage, evidently alludes to the Phansigars or Thugs.

" Though the road I have been speaking of from " Delhi to Agra be tolerable, yet hath it many " inconveniences. One may meet with tigers, " panthers, and lions upon it, and one had best also " have a care of robbers, and above all things not " to suffer any body to come near one upon the "_road. The cunningest robbers in the world are " in that country. They use a certain slip with a " running noose, which they can cast with so much " sleight about a man's neck, when they are within " reach of him, that they never fail, so that they " strangle him in a trice. They have another " cunning trick also to catch travellers with. They " send out a handsome woman upon the road, who " with her hair dishevelled seems to be all in tears, " sighing and complaining of some misfortunes " which she pretends has befallen her. Now, as " she takes the same way that the traveller goes, " he easily falls into conversation with her, and " finding her beautiful, offers her his assistance, " which she accepts ; but he hath no sooner taken " her up behind him on horseback, but she throws " the snare about his neck and strangles him, or at " least stuns him, until the robbers (who lie hid)

Purheeara. All Bundeleund and the Saugor and Nurbudda territories were supplied with the seed from whieh all their gangs arose from this great store-room. Some were Brahmans, some were Mussulmans, but all men whose aneestors had been Thugs for many generations, and being themselves fully initiated and noted men, they formed new gangs with great faeility wherever they went. W. H. S.

" come running into her assistance and complete
" what she hath begun.* But besides that, there
" are men in those quarters so skilful in casting the
" snare, that they succeed as well at a distance as
" near at hand ; and if an ox or any other beast
" belonging to a caravan run away, as sometimes
" it happens, they fail not to catch it by the neck."†

Travellers in the south of India also are sometimes decoyed through the allurements of women
into situations where they are murdered and plundered by persons lying in wait for them ; but
whether by that class of criminals who are properly called Phansigars, I am uncertain.‡ This
method, as well as that of administering intoxicat-
ing and poisonous mixtures to travellers, though
inconsonant with the habits of the large gangs
who are not accompanted in their excursions by
women, may perhaps be resorted to by smaller and
more needy parties, who rob near to their own
abodes, or who having no fixed habitation, con-
tinually roam with their families from place to
place.§

How long the country south of the Kistna has

* This may have been the case in the sixteenth century, but is
so no where now I believe. The Thugs who reside in fixed habitations and intermarry with other people, never allow their women
to accompany them or take any part in their murders. The only
exception to this rule that I am aware of is the wife of Bukhtawur
Jemadar of Jypore, after whom we have been long searching in
vain.   W. H. S.

† Thevenot's Travels, part III. page 41.

‡ The wandering bands of Thugs, who seem to retain the usages
of their ancestors, are assisted by their women in all their operations, I believe.   W. H. S.

§ I have mentioned that bands of thieves in the disguise of
Gosaens and Byragies are to be found in all parts of India ; and
these men often commit murder, and generally after stupifying
their victims with Dutera and other drugs. Other bands wander
about as Benjaras, Khunjurs, Nats, &c. &c. &c.   W. H. S.

been infested by Phansigars I know not, though it is certain that they have been settled in the Poliums of Chittoor for at least a century. On this point the Phansigars themselves are quite ignorant, knowing in general little more than that their fathers and grandfathers followed the same horrid employment, and taught it to their children. There is however no reason to suppose that the practice in this part of India is of great antiquity. It may also be a question whether to the Hindus or to the Musselmans ought to be considered as attaching the reproach of inventing this detestable system of pillage and murder. The respect paid by Musselman Phansigars to the omens and modes of divination, and to the religious and idolatrous rites of the Hindus—a respect apparently not accidental, but which pervades and seems interwoven with their whole system—affords grounds for the belief, that to them, rather than to the Musselmans, is to be ascribed the invention.*

On the other hand it may be argued, that had these bands of murderers consisted primarily of Hindus, it would probably have appeared that the practice was of considerable antiquity ; in which case there could hardly have been that prevailing ignorance among the Hindus with regard to it, which is found to exist. It is a practice more in unison with the habits and customs of the Musselmans than with those of the Hindus. The gangs at least in the southern parts of India, consist chiefly of Musselmans, and similar practices it appeared,

---

* It seems to me quite clear, that the system had its origin in some bands of robbers who had become Musselmans, and who infested the roads about Delhi above two centuries ago—that they came from the north-west, but from what country I cannot venture to guess. W. H. S.

prevailed in Hindustan in the time of Shah Jehan
and Aurung Zeb, and probably much anterior to
the reigns of these monarchs, and have continued
to the present day ; and if, as I have been informed,
Arabia and Persia be infested by Phansigars, little
room is left to doubt that these murderers came
along with the Mohammedan conquerors into India,
and that they have followed the progress southward
of the Mohammedan arms. In support of this
opinion it may be observed, further, that in the
more southern provinces which were never, or
which fell latest, a prey to Mohammedan conquerors, Phansigars do not appear even yet to have
established themselves. I have not heard of any
gangs being found to the south of Salem in Bara-
mahal; and even these there is reason to believe,
but recently migrated thither from the Poliums of
Chittoor and the Zillah of Cuddapah. With respect
to the Hindu usages, adverting to the disposition
observable among the lower orders of both nations
to adopt the rites and customs of each other, they
may have been introduced and eagerly received
among ignorant and superstitious offenders, ever
prone to embrace a scheme which serves the purpose of tranquillizing the mind without requiring
the abandonment of criminal habits either by Hindu
converts to Islamism, or by such Hindu criminals
as retaining their religion, attached themselves to
bands of Phansigars.

SUCH is Dr. Sherwood's account of Thuggee, so
far as it was known in 1816. We now proceed to
bring under the notice of the reader the circum-

stances in the condition and the customs of India, which favoured the practices of these murderers, and afforded them the means of concealment. Among these circumstances the usual mode of travelling in that country is the most remarkable and important in its relation to this matter.

Such conveniences as stage coaches,* public wagons, and boats, (excepting the Ganges steamers just established by government,) do not exist. There are not even any conveyances which a person may hire from stage to stage, unless in a very few parts of the country, where a traveller might, for a short distance, be supplied at each stage with a pony which would go at the rate of about three miles an hour ; and he could hire a few porters to carry his baggage. The only attempt at any thing like travelling posts is by going in a palkee (*Anglicè*, palanquin) carried by bearers.

Travelling *dâk*, or in a palanquin, is a mode of conveyance only available to the rich. A palkee holds but one, and the charge is never less than one, sometimes two, shillings a mile, as dear as posting in England. The traveller is obliged to give from two to five days' notice to the post-master, according to the distance ; and the average rate of proceeding is about four miles an hour.

In ordinary journeying in- India, the traveller is obliged to carry every thing with him. If a rich man is accompanied by his family, his goings forth are like those of the patriarchs of old, with his "flocks and herds, his camels, and his beasts of burden, his men-servants and his maid-servants;" he travels on his own horses, or on an elephant, while his tents, beds, cooking vessels, &c. &c., are

* See Foreign Quarterly Review No. XLI.

carried on camels or in carts. Some of his attendants accompany him on horseback, or on ponies; and the rest walk, at the rate of ten or twelve miles a day. Should he travel by water, he hires a comfortable boat for himself and his family, with as many more as he requires for his kitchen and baggage, and embarks with all his retinue. Individuals of less wealth convey their property in a few carts, and are content to sleep and eat under the shelter of trees, or of one of those magnificent groves, mango and others, which are found at a few miles interval in many parts of India. According to the rank or wealth of the individual, his mode of travelling and number of attendants varies; some have only a pony to carry their baggage, while they walk on foot; and the poorest not only walk, but carry their own stores, consisting of a blanket or quilt for a bed, a pot of brass or copper tinned* to boil pulse in or make a curry, a smaller one to drink out of, and a round plate of sheet-iron, on which, supported by two stones or lumps of earth, and with a few sticks or a little cow-dung underneath for fuel, he bakes his cakes of unleavened bread, which is merely flour and water, kneaded for a few minutes. Merchants who have goods to despatch hire either boats, carts, camels, pack-horses, or bullocks, to convey their wares to their destination; and the same conveyances, and the same drivers or conductors, proceed the whole distance, although it may be five hundred or even a thousand miles. Large sums of treasure or jewellery, amounting sometimes to several thousand pounds at a time, are constantly dispatched by the

* It is a curious distinction between the Hindoos and Mussel- mans, that the former all use brass vessels, the latter those made of copper tinned.

bankers of one town to their correspondents at several hundred miles distance, by the hands of common porters. These men, instead of going in large parties well armed, usually travel in small numbers, without any arms whatever; trusting for protection to the appearance of utmost poverty which they assume. They, however, often fall victims to the ruthless vigilance of the Thugs.

There are but few inns or serais in India; the best of them consist but of a quadrangle of arches or arcades. Some of these, raised under the Mohammedan princes, are beautiful specimens of Oriental architecture, with lofty gateways and battlements; but the greater part are more like what are built on the foundation of a new street in London, to be afterwards converted into cellars. Under the native rulers, these buildings were rather numerous and kept in tolerable order; a regular establishment of guards and servants was maintained at them; and there were private doors and apartments for women. Our readers, who are familiar with Oriental tales and the Arabian Nights, will remember them, under the name of caravan-serais or khans, as the scene of so many of the adventures therein described. Under the extortion of the earlier English government in India, however, and the consequent impoverishment of the country, all have suffered, more or less, and many of the most splendid are gone entirely to ruin. There are generally a few shops within the square; and, in places of considerable thoroughfare, a few people of a class called Buttearas, who cook dinners for travellers. Where there are no serais, travellers sleep in the verandahs of houses or in any open sheds they can find; but the climate of India is

such as not to render shelter necessary for nine
months in the year; and none but single travellers
or very small parties care for serais or houses. All
who are rich enough to carry tents, or those who
travel in tolerable numbers, usually prefer encamp-
ing under the shade of trees, at some distance from
the dirty serais or villages; and when one party is
so encamped under a shady grove, a single traveller, or even several together, will easily be induced
to join them, and often ask permission to do so, for
the sake of protection.

It is the existence of such customs which renders
the operations of the Thugs so practicable.

Our readers will almost deem it impossible that
such organised gangs of murderers, amounting to
several thousands, could carry on their villainy
almost undiscovered so long; for two or three
centuries at least.   The difficulty, however, nearly
vanishes when we reflect on the mode of travelling
in India, just described, and on the peculiar system
of the Thugs.   In the first place they seldom murder near their own homes; but even this would be
a point of little importance when we consider,
secondly, that travellers, and generally from a
distant part of the country, are their victims:
thirdly, that they invariably murder before they
rob.

Lastly, they avoid exciting suspicion by being
careful to leave behind them no marks even of a
crime having been committed.   The travellers
who became their victims were men seeking for
service; or returning home with the savings of
years; merchants going on business to a distant
town; or others journeying either for business or
pleasure. They might be murdered in the morning

twilight within half a mile of the serai or village in which they had passed the night; while the Thugs who watched and had marked them for their prey were encamped at a short distance. No one missed them : the people of the serai or village which they had left took it for granted that they had proceeded on their way; and those of the next halting-place in advance were ignorant of their approach. It is not till days, weeks, months, or even years had passed away that their relations, hearing nothing of their arrival at their intended destinations, make inquiries, and it is seldom that they can ascertain even the place about which the travellers were probably murdered. Unless the inquiry be made within a short time, and there may have been something in the appearance or equipage of the travellers to attract attention, the villagers and others who reside along the road would not recollect whether those inquired for had passed or not. But even supposing (as has occasionally occurred) that the relations succeed in tracing the travellers to a certain spot, beyond which all clue is lost; this gives a moral certainty that they have been murdered at no great distance, that is, within a few miles adjacent.—But how, within such a space, are they to pitch upon the spot where the . bodies are interred?—and more,—where are the murderers? probably hundreds of miles away; and even should they by chance be again encamped on the very spot, what means are there of detection? In ordinary thefts, and by local thieves, the tracing and discovery of stolen property affords a very powerful means of bringing the matter home to the perpetrators; but this has but little effect against Thugs. They contrive to obtain full knowledge of the persons, residence, and destination of those they murder, and are careful not to dispose of any recognisable articles where they might by chance be perceived. Such as have any peculiar marks are destroyed. .

Considering all these circumstances, it is not astonishing that so little has been done towards suppressing this association of miscreants. The fact is, that until these five or six years, no one had any correct notion of its extent: all that was known up to that period was, that travellers were occasionally enticed and murdered by people called Thugs, who assumed the garb of inoffensive wayfarers. By some extraordinary chance, such as one of the victims having made his escape, or some of the stolen property being unexpectedly recognised, or one of the gang having turned informer in consequence of a quarrel for the division of the spoil, a few of these miscreants were occasionally discovered and punished. Even had the various governments into which India is divided, been aware of the extent of the evil and anxious to destroy it, they would have been unable to do so: insulated efforts would have produced little or no benefit; the jealousies which existed would have prevented their combining for the purpose; and for a century and a half or more, there has not existed any paramount power which could devise a general plan of operations, and compel the rest to submit to it.

Other causes are not wanting which tended to prevent any attempts being made, even in detail, to arrest the proceedings of the different gangs of Thugs. Some of the native chiefs knowingly harboured and protected them as a source of revenue from which they derived considerable sums annually out of the profits of their plunder. The

Thugs lived in villages like other people, and generally cultivated small portions of ground to maintain appearances : so that the native chiefs, if questioned, pretended of course to know nothing of their real character ; asserting that these people lived, cultivated, and paid their rent like others, and accounting for the absence of most of the male population during several months, by saying that they went for service and returned periodically with the amount of their earnings. In other cases, native chiefs who would have readily punished a gang of thieves when apprehended, were deterred from doing so by superstitious dread. The Thugs always endeavoured to impress the belief that they were acting according to the injunctions of their deity Bhowanee, and that all who opposed them would feel the vengeance of their goddess. The few instances in which Thugs were put to death by native chiefs were generally cases of personal vengeance, because these villains had murdered some relation or dependent of the chief, and were by good fortune apprehended immediately, " in the red-hand." It has unfortunately in several instances occurred that after punishing Thugs, the chief himself, his son, or some relation has died within a short time : whether some of the Thug fraternity took secret means to insure such an occurrence, cannot be ascertained ; but they seized all such opportunities to substantiate the belief which they endeavoured to inculcate. In general, a native chief would merely extort a sum of money from the Thugs, or keep them in confinement for a short time, after which they were released ; and not unfrequently they were discharged at once. Their own superstition however, as has just been explained, is now beginning to operate against them.

The following will show what extraordinary proceedings occur sometimes in India. A dispatch of dollars to the value of four thousand pounds sterling, made on account of a rich merchant of Indoor, Dhun Raj, was carried off by Thugs, who murdered the attendant guards, near a place called Burwaha Ghaut, on the Nerbudda. He contrived to ascertain who the Thugs were, and, being a man of considerable influence, to occasion their arrest and detention in gaol by the native chiefs in whose jurisdiction they lived: after some time an agreement was made with the Thugs to release them, if they would refund the money or its amount.

Some paid out of the fruits of former expeditions, others borrowed in anticipation of future success; and those who had neither money nor credit, pledged themselves to pay part of their future earnings.

The Thugs durst not break their engagements for fear of Dhun Raj, and after some time he realized the full sum of which he had been plundered. Finding, however, that he could turn his power and influence to so good an account, he began to assume the character of a patron of Thugs: he had always some of the principal leaders about his person, and yearly exacted large sums of money from the principal gangs in return for his protection, threatened those who refused with arrest and punishment: and such was his influence, that he could procure the release of a gang from almost any gaol in central India.

Though the British Indian government was free from the superstitions or the corruptions which prevented the native chiefs from punishing Thugs, it was not the less hampered by prejudices of its own, and by real difficulties which lay in the way of the object desired. Regarding the prejudices alluded to, it is necessary to explain a little of the secret springs that actuated the government. The members at the head of the administration have always had a tolerably correct idea of the oppressive nature of the British rule in India, and of the light in which it is held by the natives; but it has always been a primary object to prevent this knowledge from reaching the English public. To effect this, the reports forwarded to the Court of Directors, have always descanted on the admirable system of internal government which has been established in their territories; the blessings which the native subjects enjoy; and their consequent gratitude. The feeling descends through the various ranks of government servants, who generally take their cue accordingly. It may be observed too, that the majority of the officers of government, civil or military, are extremely ignorant of the natives of India, and of their real sentiments; and are therefore easily misled by a few designing favourites, who alone possess their ear, and have their own ends to serve.

To acknowledge, even had they been fully aware of it, the existence of such an evil as Thuggee over the whole of the British provinces, was by no means agreeable to the government, it would have contradicted their repeated assertions and representations. If an evil could be suppressed quietly and without incurring any additional expense, it would have been a source of deep satisfaction; but the proceedings of government have almost warranted a belief that they would prefer the existence of an evil, provided it were not generally known, even to the discovery of a remedy, if this should tend to produce a considerable sensation and excite inquiry. We could at least instance several public officers who have brought considerable annoyance upon themselves by too broadly bringing to notice the existence of evils, or the enormous extent to which crimes of the deepest dye, such as murders, gang robbery, and others, are perpetrated. Appearances are, however, kept up. The zeal and ability of the officer are praised, and his praiseworthy motives duly appreciated;—but then come certain remarks indicating an " apprehension of his being misin- formed ;" doubts that " the evil is not so bad as he has represented;" with a concluding observation that copies of the correspondence will be sent to the superintendent of police, judge of circuit, or some superior officer, who will be desired to report on the subject. This individual, if he have any tact, or any thing to hope or fear from the favour of government, frames his report according to what he sees is wished or expected from him ; states the district to be not in worse order than others (which perhaps is true enough, owing to the vigorous mea- sures of the magistrate in question, by which crime has been abated); and, by a careful adjustment of words and phrases, contrives to do away entirely with the impression which, in accordance with truth, ought to have been received. Occasionally, where the magistrate has persisted in his represen- tations, the affair has actually ended by his remo- val, while his successor has reaped the full benefit of his exertions, and gained the entire credit of them.

A strong instance of the way in which the ends of justice may be defeated by a mistaken anxiety in public officers to gain a good name with the government by making it appear that crime does not exist, occurred in the district of Chupra in 1827. Two men were murdered by a gang of Thugs, who, almost immediately after, got drunk and quarrelled. Four of them in consequence gave information against the others, who were arrested with the property of the murdered men in their possession; these were committed for trial, and the four first allowed to turn King's evidence. The state of the case is as follows:—There was, first, the evidence of the approvers; second, the deposition of the wives of the men, who swore to the property found; and thirdly, the men accused of being Thugs could give no satisfactory account of themselves. The defence was merely a denial, and an assertion that the property claimed by the widows was their (the prisoners') own. The judgment given will scarce be credited by our readers. The prisoners were released; the approvers and the police were severely punished for perjury and for oppression; government was led to believe that no such crime as Thuggee existed in that part of the country; and the magistrate, Mr. Pringle, who had been active in apprehending many Thugs, and had reported the same, received a severe reprimand.

One fact yet remains to be mentioned, which will show the difficulties of the case. The judge, Mr. Elliot, ordered the property which was claimed by the widows to be retained in court, while all the rest of the property found on the prisoners was returned to them. Now, for whom was the above to be retained? It could not belong to any third person, but either to the prisoners or to the murdered men. If the judge disbelieved the whole story for the prosecution, and deemed the prisoners innocent, he should have restored to them this property along with the rest that was found upon them, and which they claimed as their own. If he believed the statement of the widows, that those things belonged to their husbands, then must the prisoners have been punished as the murderers, and the property would have been given to the widows. This little fact is one of those which either show a strange perversion of judgment, or denote a vacillation of mind indicating that the judge himself felt that all was not right in the orders he gave.* The truth of all that was stated on the part of the prosecution has since been fully proved by depositions of other Thug approvers; and not only so, but that Thuggee existed to a great extent in those districts, at the very time that Mr. Elliot was assuring government that no such crime occurred.

Many of the English magistrates were actuated by the same feelings. Some would not allow that Thuggee could exist in their districts, and even were excessively indignant at such statements being made by the officers employed in the suppression of this crime: they were perfectly astounded, when men dispatched by those officers proceeded to dig up the bodies of persons recently murdered in various places, sometimes within a short distance of the police functionary's residence. Others admitted that such a thing might occur occasionally ; while a few boldly and openly stated what they had discovered, and gave much valuable information. Our limits do not permit us to add here, extracts from the official papers: we must,

---

* No mention of this order to retain that portion of the property is to be found in Capt. Sleeman's book. We derive it from a statement publicly made by Mr. Pringle.

therefore, refer our readers to various letters from Mr. Wright, a Madras magistrate.

But even if all the English magistrates in India had been aware of and cordially co-operated with each other, they would have effected little towards the suppression of Thuggee. The ordinary tribunals and modes of proceeding, which answered in some degree for the detection and punishment of ordinary offenders, were of little avail against Thugs. Except in the rare instance of a gang being apprehended with stolen property in possession, which the relations of the murdered persons were there to identify, the only witnesses who could ever be brought against them were some of their own fraternity; and the evidence of men whose preliminary step must be to confess themselves the most ruthless villains in existence, is naturally received with distrust, of which the case commemorated by Mr. Pringle is a memorable example, and doubtless may plead for the judge.

Such being the English mode of proceeding, it is no wonder that approvers and informers were slow to come forward; for no sooner did they lose the protection of the functionaries, than they were murdered by their accomplices. The dilatoriness and inefficiency of the courts; the great power which the subordinate police and court officers possess to disguise the real merits of a case; the influence which the Thugs contrived to obtain over these by means of bribes; the few instances in which stolen property or bodies were discovered; all conspired to increase the difficulty under which the ordinary magistrates laboured in detecting the perpetrators of this crime. But even where the bodies were found in wells, which was a common way of disposing of them when in a hurry or likely to be disturbed, in the Doab, Oude, and other parts, the owner of the ground and his neighbuors generally buried them as quickly as possible that the police officers might know nothing of the matter; and if these did become acquainted with the circumstance, a bribe would usually prevent their reporting it to the magistrate.   The farmers and others had just grounds for what they did, owing to the ;strange mode in which the English government conducts its police affairs.   In such cases as those now mentioned the common practice is to summon to court the owners of the neighbouring lands, and many of the neighbours;—at a distance, perhaps, from ten to eighty miles, and to fine them severely as a matter of course, if they could not produce the perpetrators of the murders.

But even when an insulated gang was actually brought to justice, it was but a drop in the ocean towards the suppression of Thuggee :—nor would, nor will any thing effect this, but a general system, which shall be in operation all over India.   Different magistrates might receive information which, if it were combined and compared together, might prove of the greatest value, but which becomes useless when frittered away among separate officers, who have no communication with each other.   The whole business too was so little understood, that few could bring themselves to credit the extent of such an organized system of murder.   Although sufficient was known, so far back as 1810, to induce the commander-in-chief to issue a general order to the native soldiery who went on leave, urging them to take bills on the different treasuries for the amount of their savings, instead of carrying cash for fear of being robbed on the road, yet year after year passed, and men did not join their corps: but it was always supposed they had deserted, and little suspicion apparently was entertained of their being murdered, which however, was since discovered to have been the case in almost every instance. The scattered residences of the Thugs was another obstacle, and rendered them much more difficult to deal with than ordinary criminals, who inhabit the same locality. The members of a single gang often came from different parts of the country, some of which were hundreds of miles asunder. Numbers of them, perhaps the greater part, were residents of foreign states over which the magistrates had no control; and, although the British government might have requested the co-operation of the different princes, little or no good would have been effected. Even a system of Thug police, such as has now been established, if confined to the British provinces, could have been of no permanent use. The Thugs would have emigrated for the time to the native states, and although the crime might for a while cease in the British territories, as soon as the special Thug police was abolished, those miscreants would all have returned and prosecuted their trade as vigorously as ever.

Occasionally when a gang, residents of a foreign territory, were arrested, and moral proof against them was strong, but legal proof, according to the English system, failing; if the government made them over to their native chief in the hope that he would punish them, this usually ended in their being released by paying a sum of money—sometimes without. On the other hand, when British subjects were apprehended on a Thug expedition in a native state, they sometimes contrived, by flattering English prejudices, to obtain the protection of the functionaries. The established creed of the government is the superior excellence of their own administration, and the blessings enjoyed by their native subjects; and they descant largely on the tyranny 'and oppression in all native states. This is well known to the native dependents and. officials, who play their part accordingly. With many of them the Thugs maintained a good understanding, and when any of those wretches, residents of British territories, were arrested by a native chief, a pitiable story was presented to some English functionary of "poor innocent British subjects on a trading expedition," or something of the sort, having been confined by a tyrannical chief, in order to extort money from them. _Of course, a due proportion of compliments and flattery of the English was mixed up with the representation, and this would produce, often without the slightest inquiry, a strong letter from the English functionary to the native chief on the injustice of his proceedings, and generally insured the release of the Thugs.

MEASURES OF THE BRITISH GOVERNMENT IN INDIA FOR THE SUPPRESSION OF THUGGEE.

We now proceed to notice the measures taken by the British authorities in India for the suppression of Thuggee. The writer in the Foreign Quarterly Review, upon whose authority as well as that of Captain Sleeman, the following statements are made, seems to have had access to the most authentic original sources of information.

The state of society in India being such as we have just described, it is not surprising that so well organized a system of murder and robbery as that of the Thugs should have remained so long in full vigour.

* Things had gone on in this way for years, chequered occasionally by the vigorous attempt of some individual functionary to eradicate the evil, but without any solid benefit. The most notorious of these efforts was an attack made by Messrs. Halhed and Stockwell, in the year 1812, on the stronghold of a large body of Thugs, in the province of Sindouse, in the Gualior territory. They had formed a large village there, whence they issued annually on their excursions, and paid a regular tribute to that state for their protection. Many were killed; but the greater part, being driven away, scattered themselves all over India, joining other gangs or forming new ones wherever they went: so that the enterprize, from not being followed up on a system of information derived from some of those who were captured, actually in its results produced more evil than good.

The next event which occurred, and which ultimately laid the foundation of the successful measures that have been since pursued, was the arrest of a gang of a hundred and fifteen, near Jubulpoor, in 1823; it was accomplished by the following means. A noted leader of Thugs, named Kulian, was in the Jubulpoor gaol. Seeing the proof strong against him, he offered to turn informer to save himself; and was promised his life in the event of his doing good service. He accordingly desired his brother, Motee, to accompany the first large gang he should meet, travelling in that direction; to note well the murders and places where the bodies should be buried: and, as the gang

* For. Quart. Rev. No. xli.

6*

approached Jubulpoor, to give information to Mr.
Molony, agent to the governor-general. The gang
which Motee joined was that of Dhunnee Khan:
he strictly fulfilled his instructions, and caused the
apprehension of the whole; this has been already
related ; and also how Dhunnee Khan contrived to
persuade Mr. Molony to order their release. In
despair at this, Motee followed the gang,' and, by
dint of frightening some of them with assurances
of speedy re-apprehension, persuaded a few to
return with him to Mr. Molony, and declare what
they really were. On this additional evidence, a
large police force was sent after the gang, and
succeeded in capturing a hundred and three, who
were safely lodged in gaol. Mr. Molony unfortunately died soon after this: his successor apparently
did not know how to proceed in the case, until Mr.
F. C. Smith took it up in 1830, shortly after his
appointment as governor-general's agent at Jubulpoor; seventy-five were convicted; the others
having died in gaol, excepting some who were
made informers.

Another considerable gang was apprehended in
the same territories in 1826 by Captain Wardlow,
employed there as a civil officer ; a third by Captain Sleeman, in Bhopal, in the beginning of 1830;
and a fourth by Major Borthwick, political agent
of Mahidpoor.

Of all these gangs, some of the members, frightened at what had already occurred, turned approvers, in order to save themselves; but the evidence
of these men, in particular of a Brahmin approver,
named Ferringhea, was perfectly astounding, and
laid open a scene of barefaced villainy which could
scarcely be credited : nevertheless, every statement

hitherto made by them, and by others, have been corroborated.

The disclosures made by these different approvers, and the information given, threw open so fine a field for a general plan of operations, that the matter was warmly taken up by Mr. Smith, agent to the governor-general, and Captain Sleeman, district officer of Nursingpoor, each zealously co-operating with the other. On the 21st September, 1830, Mr. Smith wrote to government, and intimated the necessity of some such plan : but the eyes of the latter had been opened, and before the receipt of Mr. Smith's dispatch, a letter from government, dated 8th October, was addressed to him, requesting his opinion on the subject. In reply, he submitted a plan, of which the following is an outline.

1st. That an officer, to be termed superintendent of operations against Thuggee, should be appointed, with power to send out parties to apprehend those against whom he might have information in any part of the country.

2d. The superintendent to commit all whom he deems guilty for trial, before the governor-general's agent in the Saugor and Nerbudda territories.

3d. Lists to be made out against all upon whom suspicion rests, and sent to the different English functionaries.

4th. The residents at native courts also to give their assistance.

The draught likewise contains several minor provisions regarding the search for dead bodies ; rewards to those who deserve such a mark of approbation ; penalties for harbouring Thugs ; prevention of abuses by approvers ; and other clauses not worth enumerating here, although highly useful in practice.

The suggestions were, however, but partially adopted by government, for unfortunately Lord William Bentinck, at that time at the head of affairs, was not in the habit of indulging in a general or comprehensive view of any question; and his mind, while in India, was chiefly occupied in the minor details of government and the consideration of petty economical retrenchments. Captain Sleeman was, in January, 1831, removed to Saugor district, authorized to act as superintendent, to send out parties for the arrest of Thugs, and proceed as above proposed; but he was still expected to perform all his duties as civil officer of the Saugor district, without any additional pay, such being Lord William Bentinck's system. Still under so able and indefatigable an officer as Captain Sleeman much benefit occurred, and numerous arrests were made; but it soon became evident, from the extensive-nature of the Thug operations, that more aid must be granted. Accordingly, in January, 1832, another officer was appointed to take charge of the revenue and civil duties of the Saugor district, over which Captain Sleeman then presided, leaving to the latter only the magistracy department; thus allowing him more leisure to devote to Thug affairs. Three junior officers were appointed his assistants, and detached to apprehend such Thugs as they could obtain information of.

Still, the more that was done the more seemed requisite to do. Every arrest brought to light new combinations and associations of these professed assassins, and discovered new scenes in which their dreadful trade was at work. It was obvious that nothing but a general system, undertaken by a paramount power, strong enough to bear down all opposition by interested native chiefs, could ever eradicate such well-organized villainy; and the other members of government at length succeeded in persuaded Lord William Bentinck that it was incumbent upon a government calling itself enlightened to take the lead in so good a work; and that a moderate expense would be well bestowed in suppressing an association which was causing the annual murder of some thousands of his fellow creatures. In prosecution of the extended system of operations, Captain Sleeman was in January, 1835, relieved altogether from ordinary civil duties, and appointed superintendent; and several additional officers were nominated to act under him in various parts of the country.

Jubulpoor, the residence of the agent to the governor-general in the Saugor and Nerbudda territories, was appointed Captain Sleeman's headquarters. All Thugs apprehended within those territories Jeypoor, Hyderabad, Nagpoor, and other contiguous native states, are tried by the agent at Jubulpoor. Those of Oude and Indore by the residents of those courts; and such as have committed crimes in what are called the regulation provinces, are tried by the officers who are there stationed. Operations have lately extended into Bombay, Madras, the eastern parts of Bengal, and the north westernmost parts of the Indian continent; and there is no doubt that, to ensure complete success it will be necessary to nominate additional superintendents as well as subordinate officers for each of these divisions: to which should be added functionaries specially appointed for the trial of those committed.

The success of the combined operations has been

beyond hope ; and if properly followed up, it will be almost impossible for a Thug to remain at large. The mode of proceeding is, to take the deposition of those who turn approvers, wherever this may happen to be. These men are then required to give, to the best of their recollection, a full account of every expedition on which they have been, mentioning the dates of every one, and the detail of every murder ; together with the names of those who had formed the gangs, their residence, caste, &c., &c. All this is registered in the office of the general-superintendent, and lists of those to be apprehended are sent to the different subordinate officers, who are all provided with approvers and guards. These officers also take the depositions in full of all whom they may apprehend, copies of which are sent to the general-superintendent. It is obvious that when depositions, thus taken almost simultaneously from different people hundreds of miles apart, who have had no means of collusion, and none of them expecting to be apprehended, agree in describing the same scenes and the same actors, it is obviously next to impossible to refuse belief. But another test is applied. When a Thug is arrested, he is brought direct to the officers' residence, and placed in a row between unconcerned people. The approvers, who have been detained at the stations, are then sent for singly, and required to point out any individual of the party whom they may know. If they all fix on the same individual, and their statements also agree with those previously made by others, it is impossible that better evidence can be had.

We mention this, because we are aware that a prejudice has gone forth against the mode of conducting both the previous investigations and the sessions part of the business in Thug trials. That a man who has only seen or heard the latter should have some suspicions is not surprising; for the whole evidence of events long past is given so glibly, that it appears to bear strong marks of fabrication. But in fact the sessions part of the business is the least to be relied on: if that were all a man had before him to enable him to form his judgment, few Thugs would have been punished: before the trials come on, the approvers have all been brought together; have had opportunities of seeing the prisoners, and of fabricating what tales they please. But this they dare not do; they know well that what passes in the sessions, though the actual trial, yet serves chiefly to inspect the papers and operations of the subordinate officers, in order to ascertain that all has been correctly conducted; and that in reality, the previous proceedings form the evidence mainly relied upon. The whole association of Thugs is, in fact, different from that of any other known villains in existence. Their system is such, that they are beyond the reach of the ordinary tribunals of the country, and a special system must be put in force against them. That some petty abuses have been committed, we allow. Money has occasionally been extorted from people, under threat of accusing them of being Thugs; and others, though innocent, have suffered a temporary imprisonment. But there is no system, however well organized, that may not be open to imperfections; and what are such evils as the above, which are the sum total of all that has occurred, to ridding the world of some hundreds of professed assassins.

We are fully convinced, after taking everthing into consideration, that there are no trials in which

a man may with so safe a conscience pronounce
sentence, as those of the Thugs; in proof of which
we have only to refer to the table in p. 38 of Captain Sleeman's work. No less than eleven different
functionaries, judicial and political, are there mentioned as having held Thug trials; yet the general
result is the same in all, as to the proportion found
guilty and acquitted. We could mention many
individual instances in proof of the correctness of
the information obtained and evidence brought forward, but will content ourselves with one very
striking case from Hyderabad. About eighty
Thugs had been arrested in various parts of that
kingdom by different parties of approvers; they
were collected into a gang and sent off to Jubulpoor
under a guard. As they were passing the residence of the local governor of one of the Hyderabad provinces, he gave in charge to the guard
eleven men whom he had apprehended on suspicion. The whole were safely brought to Jubulpoor;
but it so happened that the papers and documents
relating to their arrest had not been received by
the time of their arrival; and the officer commanding the guard made no report as to whence
the different men who composed the gang under
his charge had been received; they were, therefore, as a matter of course, supposed to be all
Thugs who had been arrested by the approvers.
Nevertheless the usual form was proceeded in, *i. e.*
the approvers who remained at Jubulpoor were
sent for singly to inspect the gang; all were
recognized to be Thugs excepting eleven men, of
whom the approvers said they knew nothing. On
the receipt of the documents a few days afterwards,
these eleven proved to be the party given in charge

to the guard by the local governor, with whose arrest the approvers had no concern.

The success which has attended the exertions of the officers employed to suppress this crime, has hitherto equalled the most sanguine expectations. In most parts of central India, Bundlecund, Bogle-cund, and from Allahabad to the Himalayah, Thuggee now scarcely exists: the great proof of which is, that the servants of English gentlemen, and Sepahees, who go on leave into those parts of the country, have, during the last three years, all returned in safety; whereas previously, not a year passed without many of them being missed. We mention these two classes, for their movements only can we correctly ascertain; but it is a fair inference that other natives have travelled in equal safety. There can be no doubt that if the British government will pursue vigorous measures for a few years, the system will, with proper supervision on the part of the ordinary police, be completely eradicated, never again to rise; but if exertions are slackened, and any fully initiated Thugs left at large, they would infallibly raise new gangs, and Thuggee would again flourish all over India. It is certainly incumbent on a government which assumes to itself the character of enlightened, and which is now paramount in India, to exert itself for the suppression of such an atrocious system. It is impossible to ascertain with accuracy the extent to which it has been carried annually, and, could it be done, the statement would scarcely be credited. Reckoning the number of Thugs in all India to be ten thousand, and that, on the average, each Thug murders three victims a year, this will give an amount of thirty thousand murders annually committed for many years past, of which, till lately,

scarcely any thing was known. Frightfully enormous as this may appear, it is probable that both
estimates are under the mark, which is warranted
by what appears on the trials, where, of course,
but a small portion of the crimes actually committed are proved.

In the sessions of 1836, lately held by the
Honourable F. I. Shore at Jubulpoor, two hundred
and forty-one prisoners were convicted of the murder of four hundred and seventy-four individuals, of
whose corpses three hundred and fourteen were
disinterred, and inquests held upon them.

The results have been hitherto highly satisfactory. Within these few years more than two
thousand Thugs have been arrested by the officers
attached to the Jubulpoor and Central India establishment alone. Of these about three hundred
have been made approvers; eighteen hundred and
three were committed for trial.* Of these four
hundred and nineteen were sentenced to death;
one thousand and eighty to transportation for life;†
ninety-five to imprisonment for life; leaving two
hundred and nine, who were either sentenced to
limited imprisonment, allowed to turn approvers,
died in gaol, or were otherwise disposed of. Only
twenty-one of the whole have been acquitted; and
this proves the extraordinary care with which the
cases are prepared by the officers to whom this
duty has been intrusted, and the strong nature of
the evidence adduced. We cannot but wish them
every success in exterminating a system which

* This result reaches to the year 1836, and is consequently
greater than that given in a paper of Captain Sleeman's, in a subsequent part of the work.

† These sentences are at once carried into execution, and not
commuted, as is so common in England.

spares neither sex nor age ; whose members never abandon their profession as long as they possess the power to engage in an expedition ; who watch for their prey like wild beasts or vultures ; and talk of the principal scenes of their crimes as a sportsman would of his favourite preserves. We trust also that no miserable fit of economy on the part of government may arise to thwart the measures in progress, but that every co-operation will be given to those praiseworthy exertions.

CAPTAIN SLEEMAN'S NOTICE OF THE THUGS, THEIR LANGUAGE, SUPERSTITIONS AND CUSTOMS.

WE now present the reader with the account of the Thugs, by Captain Sleeman, the Superintendent of the Thug Police. This account is prefixed by the author to his Ramaseana or Vocabulary of the Thug dialect. It brings down the history to the year 1836. The vocabulary itself will be found in the Appendix to this work.

I have, I believe, entered in this Vocabulary every thing to which Thugs in any part of India have thought it necessary to assign a peculiar term ; and every term peculiar to their associations with which I have yet become acquainted. I am satisfied that there is no term, no rite, no ceremony, no opinion, no omen or usage that they have intentionally concealed from me; and if any have been accidently omitted after the numerous narratives that I have had to record, and cases to investigate, they can be but comparatively very few and unimportant.

Their peculiar dialect the Thugs call Ramasee;

and every word entered in this Vocabulary is
Ramasee in the sense assigned to it; while but few
of them are to be found at all in any language with
which I am acquainted. Their verbs have all
Hindostanee terminations, and ¡auxiliaries, such as
Kurna to make, Lena to take, Dena to give, Jana
to go, Lana to bring, Dalna to throw.

· Different terms have often been invented for the
same thing by different gangs, situated at a great
distance from each other. Many of the members
of the seven original clans who· emigrated into
remote parts of India, after their flight from Delhi,
had, perhaps, forgotten many of the terms in use
among them before they had the means of forming
new gangs out of the rude materials around them
in their new abodes, or before their own children
became old enough to obviate the necessity of
raising new recruits from among their neighbours,
and been obliged to adopt new ones. As the new
gangs became too large to be satisfied with occasional murders upon the roads in their neighbourhood, they extended their expeditions into remote
parts, and had frequent occasions of meeting and
acting in conjunction with each other; when it
became necessary that all should become so familiarly acquainted with the different terms used by
different gangs to denote the same thing, as to be
able to use them indifferently and at the moment
when occasion required.

It is not perhaps above fifty or sixty years that
the gangs of Hindoostan have been in the habit of
frequently extending their depredations into the
districts south of the Nurbudda; and to these
depredations they were invited chiefly by the Pindaree system, which rendered the roads leading
from these districts across the Nurbudda to the

Gangetic provinces, and to Hindoostan generally, very insecure; and caused the wealth to flow by those of Surgooja and Sumbulpore; and by the remittances made in jewels and specie from Bombay and Surat, to Indore and Ragpootana after the suppression of that system under the Marquis of Hastings, and the introduction of the opium monopoly into Malwa; which created an extraordinary demand for money to be advanced to the cultivators of that article.

There are in almost all parts of India money-carriers by profession, who, though in the very lowest classes of society in point of circumstances, are entrusted by merchants with the conveyance to distant parts of enormous sums in gold and jewels; and sent without a guard, and often without arms to defend themselves. Their fidelity, sagacity, and beggarly appearance are relied upon as a sufficient security; and though I have had to investigate the cases of, I may say hundreds, who have been murdered in the discharge of their duty, I have never yet heard of one who betrayed his trust. It was generally by these men, that the merchants of Bombay and Surat sent their remittances in gold and jewels through Kandeish and Malwa to Indore and Rajpootana; and from the year 1824, to the commencement of our operations in 1830, the sums taken from them by gangs of Thugs from Hindoostan, or countries north of the Nurbudda were immense. Of the following sums, we have authentic records.

1826, at Choupara on the Taptee—murder of 14 persons at one time, and plunder of - - - - 25,000 *Rs.*

1827, Malagow in Kandeish—murder of
   7 persons at one time, and plunder of - 22,000 .
1828, Dhorecote in Kandeish—murder of
   3 persons at one time, and plunder of - 12,000
1828, Burwahagat on the Nurbudda—
   murder of 9 persons at one time, and
   plunder of   -   -   -   - 40,000
1829, Dhorec in Kandeish—murder of 6
   persons at one time, and plunder of -' 82,000
1830, Baroda—murder of 25 persons, and
   plunder of   -   - '   -   - 10,000

In the Choupara affair, 150 Thugs were engaged,
and of these there. are only 33 at large. In the
Burwahaghat affair, 125 were engaged, and of
these only 12 are now at large. In the Dhoree
affair, 150 were engaged, and of these only 30 are
now at large. In the Dhorecote affair, 125 were
engaged, and of these 25 only are at large. In the
Dholeea and Malagow affair, 350 were either
present or within a stage or two of the place and
shared in the booty, and of these only 36 are now
at large.*

There are Thugs at Jubulpore from all quarters
of India;- from Lodheeana to the Carnatic, and
from the Indus to the Ganges. Some of them have
been in the habit of holding, what I may fairly call
unreserved communication with European gentlemen for more than twelve years; and yet there is
not among them one who doubts *the divine origin
of the system of Thuggee*—not one who doubts, that

---

* Total 136, but in reality there are only 69 of the Thugs
engaged in these affairs now at large, as many were engaged in
more than one of them. The total number engaged would appear
to be 900, but in reality there were only between 500 and 600 for
the same reason.

he and all who have followed the trade of murder
with the prescribed rites and observances, were
acting under the immediate orders and auspices of
the Goddess Devee, Durga, Kalee or Bhawanee,
as she is indifferently called, and consequently there
is not one who feels the slightest remorse for the
murders which he may, in the course of his voca-
tion, have perpetrated or assisted in perpetrating.
A Thug considers the persons murdered precisely
in the light of victims offering up to the Goddess;
and he remembers them, as a Priest of Jupiter
remembered the oxen, and a Priest of Saturn the
children sacrificed upon their altars. He meditates
his murders without any misgivings, he perpetrates
them without any emotions of pity, and he remembers them without any feelings of remorse. They
trouble not his dreams, nor does their recollection
ever cause him inquietude in darkness, in solitude,
or in the hour of death.

I must at the same time state that I have very
rarely discovered any instance of what may, perhaps, be termed *wanton cruelty*; that is pain inflicted beyond what was necessary to deprive the
person of life—pain either to the mind or body.
The murder of women is a violation of their rules
to which they attribute much of the success against
the system, because it is considered to have given
offence to their patroness; but no Thug was ever
known to offer insult either in act or in speech to
the women they were to murder. No gang would
ever dare to murder a woman with whom one of
its members should be suspected of having had
criminal intercourse. In Bengal, Behar, and Or-
rissa, and in the countries east of the Jumna and
Ganges, they have not I believe yet ventured to
violate this rule against the murder of females;

and in the countries south of the Nurbudda river they have rarely violated it, I am told, except in the case of old women whom they could not conveniently separate from parties of travellers, or whom they supposed to be very wealthy. The gangs who inhabited the countries between the rivers Indus, Jumna, and Nurbudda, are the only ones that have yet ventured to murder women indiscriminately; and the belief that they owe their downfall in great measure to their having done so, will effectually prevent the practice from extending to other countries. The Thugs who resided between the Ganges and Jumna, did not, however, much scruple to participate in the murder of females while associated with the gangs of Bundelcund and Gwalior in their expeditions to the west of the Jumna, and south of the Nurbudda.

I have never found a Thug by birth, or one who had been fully initiated in its mysteries, who doubted the *inspiration of the pick-axe,** when consecrated in due form,—not one who doubted that the omens described in this work were all-sufficient to guide them to their prey, or to warn them from their danger; or that they were the signs ordained by the Goddess expressly for these purposes,—not one who doubted, that if these omens had been attended to, and the prescribed rules observed, the system of Thuggee must have flourished under the auspices of its divine patroness, in spite of all the efforts for its suppression.

There is every reason to believe that the system of Thuggee or Phansegeeree, originated with some parties of vagrant Mahommuduns, who infested the roads about the ancient capital of India. Hero-

* See vocabulary in the Appendix, article *Kussee.*

dotus, in his Polymnia, mentions, as a part of the army with which Xerxes invaded Greece, a body of horse from among the Sagartii, a pastoral people of Persian descent, and who spoke the Persian language. Their only offensive weapons were a dagger, and a cord made of twisted leather with a noose at one end. With this cord they entangled their enemies or their horses, and when they got them down they easily put them to death. Thievenot, in the passage quoted by Doctor Sherwood from his Travels, part 3d, page 41, states,—
" Though the road I have been speaking of from
" Delhi to Agra be tolerable, yet hath it many
" inconveniences. One may meet with tygers,
" panthers, and lyons upon it ; and one had best
" also have a care of robbers, and above all things
" not to suffer any body to come near one upon
" the road. The cunningest robbers in the world
" are in that country. They use a certain rope
" with a running noose, which they can cast
" with so much sleight about a man's neck
" when they are within reach of him, that they
" never fail, so that they strangle him in a trice,
" &c. &c. But, besides that there are men in
" those quarters so skilful in casting the snare that
" they succeed as well at a distance as near at
" hand, and if an ox or any other beast belonging
" to a caravan run away, as sometimes it happens,
" they fail not to catch it by the neck."*

Now, though there is a vast interval of time between the Persian invasion of Greece and the travels of Thievenot, and of space between the seat of Sagartii and that of the ancient capital of

---

* Thievenot was born 1621—he died 1692, and his travels were published 1687.

India, I am still inclined to think that the vagrant bands, who, in the sixteenth century infested the roads, as above described, between Delhi and Agra, came from some wild tribe and country of the kind: and I feel myself no doubt, that from these vagrant bands are descended the seven clans of Mahommudun Thugs, Bhys, Bursote, Kachunee, Huttar, Ganoo, and Tundel,* who, by the,common consent of all Thugs throughout India, whether Hindoos or Mahommuduns, are admitted to be the most ancient, and the great original trunk upon which all others have at different times and in different places been grafted. Bands of these vagrants, under various denominations, are to be found in all parts of India, but are most numerous, I believe, to the north and west. They all retain in some degree their pristine habits and usages; and taking their families with them, they allow their women to assist in the murders which they perpetrate in their encampments; but they have always some other ostensible employment, and as the other Thugs, who live among and cannot be distinguished from other men, say, " they live in " the desert and work in the desert, and their deeds " are not known !"

But whatever may have been the origin of the system, it is sufficiently manifest that their faith in its divine origin is of Indian growth, and has been gradually produced by the habit of systematically confounding coincidences of circumstances and events with cause and effect. This is a weakness in some degree inherent in human nature, and

---

* Some include also the Kathur clan who are also called Ghuga-ros, but by most they are considered to be merely a sect from one of the original clans.

common, therefore, in some degree, to all states and classes of society. The man who seriously believes that he is habitually blessed with good or cursed with bad luck at cards or dice, the mother who believes that her child sickens because her friends venture to praise its freshness or its appetite, have it in common with the poor Bhoomka of the wild tracts of India, who believes that he can charm the tiger from his village, the Garpuguree who believes that he can divert the hail storm from the corn fields of its cultivators, and the Thug, who believes that he can inspire his pick-axe.* But India is emphatically the land of superstition, and in this land the system of Thuggee, the most extraordinary that has ever been recorded in the history of the human race, had found a congenial soil and flourished with rank luxuriance for more than two centuries, till its roots had penetrated and spread over almost every district within the limits of our dominions, when the present plan of operations for its suppression was adopted in 1830 by the then Governor General Lord William Bentick.

For many years up to 1829 these assassins traversed every great and much frequented road from the Himalah Mountains to the Nerbudda

* In many parts of Berar and Malwa, every village has its Bhoomka, whose office it is to charm the tigers ; and its Garpu-guree, whose duty it is to keep off the hail storms. They are part of the village servants, and paid by the village community. After a severe storm that took place in the district of Nursingpore, of which I had the civil charge in 1823, the office of Garpuguree was restored to several villages in which it had ceased for several generations. They are all Brahmans, and take advantage of such calamities to impress the people with an opinion of their usefulness. The Bhoomkas are all Gonds, or people of the woods, who worship their own Lares and Penates.

river, and from the Ganges to the Indus, without
the fear of punishment from divine or human laws.
There is not now, I believe, within that space a
single road except in the western parts of Rajpootana and Guzerat, that is not free from their depredations; and whatever may be ultimately the
opinion of thinking men regarding the general
character and results of Lord William Bentinck's
administration, I hope all will unite in applauding
the boldness which could adopt, and the firmness
which could so steadily pursue this great measure
for relieving the native society of India from an
evil which pressed on them so heavily, and on
them alone; for these assassins had rarely if ever
attacked Europeans. It was not against their
tenets to do so, but they knew that Europeans
seldom travelled with much money or other valuable property about their persons, and that their disappearance would cause much more inquiry, and
consequently more danger to their associations
than that of native travellers.

So early as April 1810 the commander-in-chief
of the army thought it necessary to issue an order,
cautioning the native troops against this dreadful
evil to which so many brave soldiers of every
regiment in the service were annually falling victims; but all attacks upon the evil itself continued
to be, as heretofore, insulated and accidental.
They were planned and executed by individual
magistrates, who becoming by accident acquainted
with the existence of the evil within their jurisdictions applied their abilities and their energies for a
time to its suppression; but their different efforts
being unconnected either in time or in place, and
often discouraged and repressed by the incredulity

of controling powers, were found ultimately almost
every where alike unavailing.*

* GENERAL ORDERS BY MAJOR GENERAL ST.
LEGER, COMMANDING THE FORCES.

Head Quarters, Cawnpore, the 28th April, 1810.

" It having come to the knowledge of Government that several
" Sepoys proceeding to visit their families on leave of absence from
" their corps have been robbed and murdered by a description of
" persons denominated *Thugs,* who infested the districts of the
" Dooab and other parts of the Upper Provinces, and the insidious
" means by which they prosecute their plans of robbery and assas-
" sination having been ascertained, the Commander of the Forces
" thinks it proper to give them publicity in General Orders to the
" end that Commanding Officers of Native Corps may put their
" men on their guard accordingly.

" It has been stated, that these murderers, when they obtain
" information of a traveller who is supposed to have money about
" his person, contrive to fall in with him on the road or in the
" Serais ; and under pretence of proceeding to the same place, keep
" him company, and by indirect questions get an insight into his
" affairs, after which they watch for an opportunity to destroy him.
" This they sometimes create by persuading the traveller to quit
" the Sarais a little after midnight, pretending it is near day-break,
" or by detaching him from his companions lead him under various
" pretences to some solitary spot.

" It appears that in the destruction of their victim they first use
" some deleterious substance, commonly the seeds of a plant called
" Duttora, which they contrive to administer in tobacco, pawn, the
" hookah, food or drink of the traveller. As soon as the poison
" begins to take-effect, by inducing a stupor or languor, they strangle
" him to prevent his crying out, when, after stripping and plun-
" dering him, the deed is completed by a stab in the belly on the
" brink of a well into which they plunge the body so instantaneously
" that no blood can stain the ground or clothes of the assassin.

" As the Company's Sepoys who proceed on leave of absence
" generally carry about them the savings from their pay in specie,
" and travel unarmed, they are eagerly sought out by these robbers
" as the particular objects of their depredation. With a view there-
" fore to guard against such atrocious deeds, the Commanding
" Officers of Native Corps will caution their men when proceeding
" on leave of absence.

1st. " To be strictly on their guard against all persons (particu-
" larly those unarmed) whom they fall in with on the road who

That truly great and good man the Marquis of Hastings, to whom India is perhaps more indebted than to any other individual whose character and station have had any influence upon its destinies, has the following passage in his short summary of his own administration of the government of India; and yet, strange to say, of the operations of that force the Gwalior Contingent, which this Nobleman supposed to have been so effectually employed in the suppression of this system, there is now to be found neither recollection nor record either among the officers who commanded it, or the people against whom it was employed. " Scindiah had " evaded producing this contingent until after the " destruction of the Pindaries. To compensate for " such a delay, which I affected to consider as

" evince a solicitude to keep them company on pretence that they "are going the same way and are inquisitive about their affairs.
2d. " Not to quit the Sarais at a very early hour in the morning " before the rest of the travellers.
3d. " Not to receive pawn, tobacco, sweetmeat, &c. &c. from " such persons, or smoke their hookahs, particularly if offered to " them in solitary spots on the road ; and lastly to avail themselves " of the protection of sowars (horsemen) when opportunity offers, " or travel as much as possible with large bodies of people. This " last object might be attained in a great degree if the men were "persuaded, on occasions of periodical leave of absence, to keep " together on the road, as long as the several destinations of such " Native Commissioned or Non-Commissioned Officers as may be " proceeding the same way will admit.
" It has also been intimated to the Major General Commanding " the Forces, that the Residents at Delhi and Lucknow, and the " Collectors of Revenue will be authorized, on the application of "Commanding Officers of Pay Masters, to grant bills payable at " sight and at the usual exchange, on any other treasury for sums " which may be paid into their own Treasuries on account of " Sepoys wishing to remit money from one point of the country to " another ; a mode which in conformity to the views of government " is particularly to be encouraged and attended to by Officers " Commanding Corps and Detachments."

" accidental, I pressed that the corps should be
" employed in extinguishing certain mischievous
" associations in Scindiah's territories. The de-
" scription applied not only to some bands of
" avowed robbers, but to a particular class denomi-
" nated Thugs. This nefarious fraternity, amount-
" ing, by the first information, to above a thousand
" individuals, was scattered through different vil-
" lages often remote from each other; yet they
" pursued with a species of concert, their avocation.
" This was the making excursions to distant districts,
" where, under the appearance of journeying along
" the high roads, they endeavoured to associate
" themselves with travellers, by either obtaining
" leave to accompany them as if for protection, or,
" when that permission was refused, keeping near
" them on the same pretext. Their business was
" to seek an opportunity of murdering the travellers
" when asleep or off their guard. In this, three or
" four could combine without having given suspicion
" of their connection. Though personally unac-
" quainted, they had signs and tokens by which
" each recognized the other as of the brotherhood ;
" and their object being understood, without the
" necessity of verbal communication, they shunned
" all speech with each other till the utterance of a
" mystical term or two announced the favourable
" moment, and claimed common effort. Scindiah's
" tolerance of an evil so perfectly ascertained,
" merely because the assassinations were seldom
" committed within his own dominions, may afford
" a tolerable notion of the vitiation of society in
" Central India before this late convulsion. There
" is reason to believe that by this time the pest in
" question has been rooted out; which, with the
" suppression of some bodies of horsemen under

"military adventurers (a service completely
"achieved by the contingent), will be no less a
"benefit to Scindiah's own government, than to
"adjacent countries."

This system has now, August, 1835, I hope, been
happily suppressed in the Saugor and Nurbudda
territories, Bhopaul, Bundelcund, Boghelcund,
Eastern Malwa, the greater-part of Gwalior, the
districts between the Ganges and the Jumna. It
has also I hope been suppressed in Candeish, Go-
zerat, Berar, Rajpootana, Western Malwa, and
the Delhi territories, in as far as it arose from the
depredations of gangs that resided in the territories
above-named, within which little more I hope
remains to be done than to collect the fragments of
the general wreck of the system—the *Burkas*, or
fully initiated Thugs, who have as yet escaped us,
and are capable of creating new gangs in any part
of India that they may be permitted to inhabit;
and that they will so create them if left for any
time undisturbed in any place, no man who is well
acquainted with the system will for a moment doubt.

But that the system has been suppressed in every
part of India where it once prevailed (and I believe
that it prevailed more or less in every part) is,
however, a proposition that neither ought nor can
be affirmed *absolutely*, for, as justly observed by
the able magistrate of Chittoor in 1812, Mr. W. E.
Wright—" with respect to the crime of murder by
"Thugs or Fanseegeers, it is not possible for any
"magistrate to say how much it prevails in his
"district, in consequence of the precautions taken
"by these people in burying the bodies of the
"murdered."* To affirm absolutely that it has

* See his letter to the Secretary to the Madras Government
dated 1st July, 1812.

been suppressed while any seeds of the system remain to germinate and spread again over the land might soon render all that has been done unavailing, for there is in it a " principle of vitality" which can be found hardly in any other; and unhappily there exists every where too great a disposition to believe that we have completed what we have only successfully begun. However honourable to the individuals engaged in it and useful to the people the duty of suppressing this evil may be considered, it certainly is one of great labour and of most painful responsibility; and as almost all those who have yet devoted their abilities to the task have done so at a personal sacrifice of some kind or another to themselves, they have naturally felt anxious to see their part of the work completed as soon as possible. " Fere libenter id, quod volunt homines, credunt," was an observation of Cæsar's, the truth of which is illustrated in almost every human undertaking; and though I do not think any public officer will declare this evil suppressed within his jurisdiction before he believes it to be so, I fear many will, as heretofore, believe it to be so, long before it really is.* There were, and I believe, still are in Bundelcund, and the districts between the Ganges and the Jumna, some small gangs of these assassins who confined their operations to the roads in the neighbourhood of their residence, and the secrets of their crimes to

---

* It has been every where found dangerous for a magistrate to make it appear to his native police officers, that he believes or wishes to believe that the crime of Thuggee has entirely ceased within his jurisdiction, for they will always be found ready to avail themselves of such an impression to misrepresent cases that might otherwise lead to discoveries of great importance. Bodies of travellers that have been strangled by Thugs have, in numerous instances, been either concealed or represented by the police as those of men

S*

their own families, or to a very small circle of friends and associates. They were either in their infancy, or formed by very shrewd old men who saw the danger of continuing with the large gangs and extending their expeditions into very distant parts. Bukshee Jemadar, one of the most noted Thug leaders of his day, who died in the Saugor jail in 1832, had for some fifteen years ceased to accompany the large gangs, and was supposed to have left off the trade entirely. He was settled at Chutterpore on the great road from Saugor to Culpee, with his three sons, all stout young men, who were supposed by all the old associates of their

who had died of disease, or been killed by tigers, and have been burned without further inquiry, when a careful inquest by impartial persons would have shown the marks of strangulation upon their neeks. Landholders of all descriptions, whether ostensibly entrusted with the police duties of their estates or not, will in the same manner always endeavour to conceal the discovery of murders perpetrated within them by these people under a magistrate anxious to believe that the crime does not exist within his division. In some parts of India heavy penalties are injudiciously imposed upon landholders and police officers within whose estates or jurisdictions bodies of murdered men may be found unless they can produce the perpetrators, which is, in effect, to encourage the crime by discouraging the report of those discoveries that might lead to the arrest and conviction of the murderers.

Mr. Wilson writes to me on the 3d December, 1834,—" It is " painful to observe that wherever the Thugs go they are invariably " protected by the Zumeendars, and the premises of the Thakurs or " principal landholders are the certain spots to find them in." This observation so just with regard to the districts east of the Jumna, has been, unhappily, found equally applicable to every other part of India to which our operations have extended. The Zumeendars or landholders of every description have every where been found ready to receive these people under their protection from the desire to share in the fruits of their expeditions, and without the slightest feeling of religious or moral responsibility for the murders which they know must be perpetrated to secure these fruits. All that they require from them is a promise that they will not commit murders within their estates, and thereby involve them in trouble.

father never to have been initiated in the mysteries
of Thuggee. They were all however arrested with
their father and brought to Saugor. A trooper of
the 10th cavalry came to me some time after this
from the Mow Cantonments with a piteous tale of
the loss and supposed murder of his younger brother,
a trooper in the same regiment, whom he had a
year or two before, while on their way to their
homes on furlough, left in company with a small
party of *extremely civil men* in the neighbourhood
of Chutterpore. The young trooper's pony *had
become lame* on the road, and his brother and party
went on to prepare their dinner, telling him to spare
his pony and come up slowly, as they would have
every thing ready for him by the time he arrived.
" The strangers had, he said, been very kind to
" him, and very solicitous about the accident to
" his pony; and promised to see him safe to the
" encampment, as they were obliged to wait for a
" relation who was following : but his brother could
" never after be found." I took the trooper at his
request to the jail, and almost as soon as he entered
he put his hand upon the shoulder of Bukshee's
youngest son, who was remarkable for his large
eyes, saying, " What did you do with my poor
brother—where did you murder and bury him?"
and turning round while he yet had hold of the
man, he said, " this is one of the men to whom I
confided my brother." Jawahir and his brothers,
who had hitherto persisted in denying that they
had ever been on Thuggee, and whose father's
old associates, now admitted King's evidences,
used to declare that this son, Jawahir, so far from
having been on Thuggee, was such a chicken-
hearted lad that the very name of murder used to
frighten him, now thought the charm had been

broken, and confessed that their father had initiated them from their boyhood; but having limited their expeditions to that road, and admitted only a small party of associates their proceedings had remained undiscovered. Some of the old members of these small gangs have been secured and convicted of old crimes perpetrated while they were associated with the large gangs, and they have in consequence suspended their operations; but they will resume them again when our pursuit ceases unless all their principal members be brought to punishment.

It has now become quite clear to every unprejudiced magistrate, that, as a general principle, he can never rely upon the landholder of a village either to assist him in the arrest of these people, or to prevent their following their trade of murder when they are made over to him upon his pledge to do so. His own particular interest in encouraging the system and sharing in the spoil, will always be dearer to him than any that he can hope to enjoy in common with the society at large by the suppression of it. When driven from one part of the country they never doubt of being soon able to secure the good will of such landholders in any other, for they find little or no difficulty in establishing themselves in new village communities, and in connecting their dreadful trade with the pursuits of agriculture. Left unmolested for a few years they gain recruits from among the youth of their neighbourhood; and by a lavish expenditure of the booty they acquire, and by that mild and conciliatory deportment which they find it necessary to learn and observe on all occasions for the successful prosecution of their trade, they very soon gain the good will of their new circle of society, and contrive to make every member feel interested in their security and success. No men observe more strictly in domestic life all that is enjoined by their priests, or demanded by their respective casts; nor do any men cultivate with more care the esteem of their neighbours, or court with more assiduity the good will of all constituted local authorities. In short, to men who do not know them, the principal members of these associations will always appear to be among the most amiable, most respectable, and most intelligent members of the lower, and sometimes the middle and higher classes of native society; and it is by no means to be inferred that every man who attempts to screen them from justice knows them to be murderers.*

* I will here quote a passage from a private letter of Mr. McLeod to me, written at Dholepore or the banks of the Chumbul, May, 23d, 1833. " I am about to send off Purusram, Lack's brother, without irons is search of his father's gang, accompanied only by a sowar, a sipahee or two, and a chuprassec of my own, all of whom will be directed to conceal their livery. They will be instructed on falling in with the gang to give intelligence at the nearest residence of a native functionary, and be furnished with a document requesting such functionary to have them seized us 'Companee ku chor,' and delivered over to his superior to whom application will afterwards be made for their transfer. Purusram states that he can, if necessary, dig up at every stage the bodies of men they have lately murdered to satisfy the scruples of such as doubt his information. That he will find out the gang I have not the slightest doubt, and if he prove as faithful and intelligent as I hope, we may safely calculate upon their seizure. To ensure his earnestness as far as possible, I have assured him that I will do my utmost to have his father pardoned, and that your assurance before leaving Saugor made me confident that he would be so. In your last you say he ought not to be spared as he has neglected your invitations, but I really doubt whether they can ever have reached him in an authentic form; for both Lack and his brother assert that such assurance is all he wants, and his old wife has just toddled away home fully confident that, if he returns *unseized*, she will speedily conduct him into my presence or that of some European officer. When we consider the indistinct account they receive of the horrors of Saugor much allowance must be made for them in this

When Feringeea,* a Thug leader of some note,
for whose arrest government paid five hundred

respect. Bhimmee Jemadar tells me that when Dureean the
runaway approver joined them, he said—"Oh! my friends you had
" better eut and run as fast as you ean—hundreds of us Thugs are
" being strung about Saugor—still more aré sent to the Blackwater,
" which is worse; and those that eseape are eut muttee* for life
" —as to the poor approvers, Sleeman Sahib is getting a large mill
" made up at the Mint to grind them all to powder." They of
eourse all took to their heels after this. Bhimmee is a mild, respectable kind of man who would eertainly not appear born for a
gallows, and I hope you will let him remain with me. I feel
interested, too, for the whole of Laek's family, among whom I do
not think there is naturally any viee, and shoeking as their pro-
eeedings would appear at home, very many palliating eireumstan-
ees evidently exist here, and we must be guided by what is
expedient. To Laek the sentenee of any of his brothers would be
most disheartening. When he heard of their arrest, he repeated
with great feeling a Hindostanee verse to this effeet. "I was a
" pearl onee residing in eomfort in the oeean. I surrendered myself,
" believing I should repose in peaee in the bosom of some fair
" damsel—but alas! they have piereed me, and passed a sting
" through my body, and have left me to dangle in eonstant pain as
" as an ornament to her nose." I will have his narrative taken
and sent to you.   D. F. M'Leod.

Lieutenant Thomas, a very talented offieer, writes to me from
Gualior 2d September, 1835—"Munohur, the brother of Leak,
(eousin not brother) has voluutarily surrendered himself, at the
persuasion of his mother, who lately sent to me for Laek: Upon
sending him to her, I told Laek that I would eertainly intereede
with you for his brother if he would plaee himself in my eustody.
He is many years younger than Laek, and has one of the most
benevolent eountenanees that I have ever seen. He looks as
though he would rather eommit suieide than eommon, and cold
blooded murder. He tells me that he ean point out the homes in
the Jypore and Jodhpore villages of many noted Sooseea Thugs;
that Raejoo is now at his home, and that he left those gangs only
a month sinee aetually on Thuggee in Jodhpore."
                                          G. P. Thomas.

          * Earth. (Ed.)

---

* This Feringeea was for several years in the service of Sir
David Oehterlony, as a *Jemadar,*—a sort of sergeant, in command
of the armed attendants of a great man.

rupees, was brought in to me at Saugor in December, 1830, he told me, that if his life were spared he could secure the arrest of several large gangs who were in February to rendezvous at Jypore, and proceed into Guzerat and Candeish. Seeing me disposed to doubt his authority upon a point of so much importance, he requested me to put him to the proof—to take him through the village of Selohda, which lay two stages from Saugor on the road to Seronge, and through which I was about to pass in my tour of the district, of which I had received the civil charge, and he would show me his ability and inclination to give me correct information. I did so, and my tents were pitched, where tents usually are, in the small mango grove. I reached them in the evening, and when I got up in the morning, he pointed out three places, in which he and his gang had deposited at different intervals the bodies of three parties of travellers. A Pundit and six attendants murdered in 1818, lay among the ropes of my sleeping tent, a Havildar and four Sipahaes murdered in 1824, lay under my horses, and four Brahman carriers of Ganges water, and a woman murdered soon after the

Purusram came up with his fathers' gang at Alneeabas in the Joudpore territory, where they had been arrested by the Thakur who refused to give them to our guard—beat the old man to death and released the rest.

Mr. Wilson, Sept. 1835, observes of Makeen Lodhee, one of the approvers, that "he is one of the best men I have ever known!" and I believe that Makeen may be trusted in any relation of life, save that between a Thug who has taken the *auspices* and a traveller who has something worth taking upon him. They all look upon travellers as a sportsman looks upon hares and pheasants; and they recollect their favourite *Beles*, or places of murder, as sportsmen recollect their best sporting grounds, and talk of them, when they can, with the same kind of glee!

Pundit, lay within my sleeping tent.* The sward
had grown over the whole, and not the slightest
sign of its ever having been broken was to be seen.
The thing seemed to me incredible; but after
examining attentively a small brick terrace close
by, and the different trees around, he declared himself prepared to stake his life upon the accuracy of
his information. My wife was still sleeping over
the grave of the water-carriers unconscious of what
was doing or to be done.† I assembled the people
of the surrounding villages, and the Thanadar and
his police, who resided in the village of Korae
close by, and put the people to work over the
grave of the Havildar. They dug down five feet
without perceiving the slightest signs of the bodies
or of a grave. All the people assembled seemed
delighted to think that I was become weary like
themselves, and satisfied that the man was derang-
ed; but there was a calm and quiet confidence
about him that made me insist upon their going on,
and at last we came upon the bodies of the whole
five laid out precisely as he had described. My
wife, still unconscious of our object in digging, had
repaired to the breakfast tent which was pitched
at some distance from the grove; and I now had
the ropes of the tent removed, and the bodies of
the Pundit and his six companions in a much
greater state of decay, exhumed from about the
same depth, and from the exact spot pointed out.
The Cawrutties were afterwards disinterred, and

---

* The principal leaders of the gangs, by whom these Brahmins
were murdered, were Brahmuns, Aman, the cousin of Feringeea,
and Dirgpaal, both Subardars of Thugs.

† She has often since declared that she never had a night of such
horrid dreams, and that while asleep her soul must consequently
have become conscious of the dreadful crimes that had been there
perpetrated.

he offered to point out others in the neighbouring groves, but I was sick of the horrid work, and satisfied with what he had already done.* The gangs which were concentrating upon Jypore were pursued, and the greater part of them taken; and Feringeea's life was spared for his services.

While I was in the civil charge of the district of Nursingpore, in the valley of the Nurbuddah, in the years 1822, 23, and 24, no ordinary robbery or theft could be committed without my becoming acquainted with it; nor was there a robber or a thief of the ordinary kind in the district, with whose character I had not become acquainted in the discharge of my duty as magistrate; and if any man had then told me, that a gang of assassins by profession, resided in the village of *Kundelee*, not four hundred yards from my court, and that the extensive groves of the village of Mundesur, only one stage from me, on the road to Saugor and Bhopaul, was one of the greatest *Beles*, or places of murder in all India; and that large gangs from Hindustan and the Duckun used to rendezvous in these groves, remain in them for many days together every year, and carry on their dreadful trade along all the lines of road that pass by and branch off from them, with the knowledge and connivance of the two landholders by whose ancestors these groves had been planted, I should have thought him a fool or a madman; and yet nothing could have been more

* The proprietor of the village of Selohda connived at all this, and received the horse of the Pundit in a present. Several of the gang resided in this village, and the rest used to encamp in his grove every year in passing, and remain there for many days at a time, feasting, carousing and murdering. The people of the village and of the surrounding country knew nothing of these transactions, nor did the police of the thana of Korac.

true. The bodies of a hundred travellers lie buried
in and around the *groves of Mundesur*; and a gang
of assassins lived in and about the village of Kundelee, while I was magistrate of the district, and
extended their depredations to the cities of Poona
and Hydrabad.

The first party of men I sent into the Duckun to
aid Captain Reynolds, who had been selected by
Colonel Stewart to superintend the employment of
our means for the suppression of the system in the
Nizam's dominions, recognized in the person of
one of the most respectable *linen drapers* of the
cantonments of Hingolee, Huree Sing, the adopted
son of Jowahir Sookul, Subahdar of Thugs, who
had twenty years before been executed with
twenty-one of his followers at Aggur for the
murder of a party of two women and eight men
close to the cantonments. On hearing that the
Huree Sing of the list sent to him of noted Thugs
at large in the Duckun was the Huree Sing of the
Sudder Bazar, Captain Reynolds was quite astounded, for so correct had he been in his deportment
and all his dealings, that he had won the esteem of
all the gentlemen of the station, who used to assist
him in procuring passports for his goods on their
way from Bombay; and yet he had, as he has
since himself shown, been carrying on his trade of
murder up to the very day of his arrest with gangs
of Hindustan and the Duckun on all the roads
around, and close to the cantonments of Hingolee;
and leading out his gang of assassins while he pretended to be on his way to Bombay for a supply of
fresh linens and broad cloth. Captain Reynolds
had for several years up to this time had the civil
charge of the district of Hingolee, without having
had the slightest suspicion of the numerous murders

that he has now discovered , to have been every year perpetrated within his jurisdiction.*

* The following is an extract from the narrative of this Hurree Sing alias Hureea, taken at Hingolee.

" A year and a half before I was arrested at Hingolee, in June, " 1832, I set up a shop in the bazar of the Golundauz in the Hingo- " lee cantonments. I used before to bring cloths from Berar to the " cantonments for sale ; and became intimately acquainted with " Maha Sing, Subahdar of the Golundauzes. I told him that I " should like to set up a shop in his bazar ; and he advised me to " do so, and got the Cotwal to assign me a place. I set up a linen " draper's shop, and I went several times with other shop-keepers " to Bombay to purchase a stock of broad cloths and other articles. " The people of the cantonments knew that I used to deal to the " extent of several hundred rupees.

" When I resided at Omrowtee about seven years ago, I used to " come to Hingolee and lodge in the house of Ram Sing, Thug, " who has since been seized and sent to Jubulpore. Sometimes I " came with the gangs on Thuggee and sometimes as a merchant " with cloths for sale. When I came with cloths I used to stay for " fifteen or twenty days at a time in the Moghul Sowar lines, and " other places. After the release of Hurnagur and his gang from " Hingolee after the Girgow murders, I, with Maunkhan, the two " Nasirs, Chotee approver and others, killed three Marwaries ; and " after this Imam and Chotee got seized at Saugor, and this was " reported to me by Kureem Khan and others who came to Om- " rowtee from the Nurbudda valley ; and I thought that I might be " pointed out and arrested. This was my reason for leaving Om- " rowtee for Hingolee. When I was arrested I had determined to " leave off Thuggee, and-intended to go and reside at Bombay. I " used to go out occasionally on Thuggee after I settled at Hingo- " lee, and when the gangs of Thugs encamped on the tank or " lodged in the Dhurumsalah, I used to converse with them ; but I " never let them know where I resided. Ismael Thug, who is now " an approver, used to reside in the bazar of the fifth regiment, and " he served Captain Scott as a Gareewan. Mohua, alias Ruhman, " used also to reside here sometimes. Bahleen also used to live and " work in the bazar, but they used all three to go on the roads, as " many travellers used to pass and no one sought after Thugs. " Any skilful party might have had three or four *affairs* every " night without any one being the wiser for it. People knew not " what Thuggee was, nor what kind of people Thugs were. Travel- " lers were frequently reported to have been murdered by robbers, " but people thought the robbers must be in the jungles ; and never " dreamed that they were murdered by the men they saw every

In Oude and other parts of India where the fields
are irrigated from wells, the bodies of travellers
murdered by these people are frequently found by
the cultivators and landholders who take them out
and bury them without any report to the police,
knowing that they are the bodies of travellers so
murdered, whose distant friends are not likely to
trouble them with any inquiries. In some instances
we have found that they save themselves this
trouble by throwing in some dead carcase in order
to account for the offensive smell of the putrid
bodies, should any one have the curiosity to inquire
the cause.   Such, in short, are the precautions
taken by these people to conceal their murders both
before and after they take place, that they may be
every year perpetrated in the district of the most
vigilant magistrate without his having any knowledge or suspicion of them; and their subsequent
discovery must not be considered to detract from
his character as a public officer unless it can be
shown that he has discouraged the free report of
those circumstances that might have led to the discovery earlier.

The extent of good above described has been
effected by the arrest of above two thousand Thugs,
who have been tried at Indore, Hydrabad, Saugor
and Jubulpore.   One hundred and fifty have been
tried and convicted at Indore, eighty-four at Hydrabad; and at Saugor and Jubulpore above twelve
hundred have been convicted, in one hundred
and sixty-seven trials, of the murder of nine
hundred and forty-seven persons; while about two

" day about them. I never invited a Thug to my house, nor did I
" ever expose any of the articles obtained in Thuggee for sale. I
" was much respected by the people of the town and cantonments
" and never suspected till arrested."

hundred and fifty have, in all these trials at Indore, Hydrabad, Saugor and Jubulpore, been admitted as King's evidences on the conditions of exemption from the punishment of death and transportation beyond seas for all past offences, provided they placed all those offences on record when required to do so, and assisted in the arrest of their associates in crime.

These men are commonly tried for one particular case of murder, perpetrated on one expedition, in which case all the gang may have participated, and in which the evidence is the most complete. On an average more than ten of these cases have been found to occur on every expedition; and every man has, on an average, been on more than ten of these expeditions. The murders for which they are tried are not, therefore, commonly more than a hundredth part of the murders they have perpetrated in the course of their career of crime. In the last sessions held at Jubulpore by Mr. Smith for 1834-35, thirty-six cases from Hydrabad, committed by Captain Reynolds, and forty-two cases from other parts committed by myself, were tried, and two hundred and six prisoners convicted of the murder of four hundred and forty persons. Of these persons the bodies of three hundred and ninety had been disinterred and inquests held upon them, leaving only fifty-five unaccounted for.*

In the dominions of the King of Oude much has already been done by Colonel Low and Captain Paton; and I have no doubt of a successful result to our efforts in that quarter provided the pursuit

* These trials included several supplementary cases, or cases which had been tried before, but were brought on as other prisoners, who were not forthcoming when they were first tried, have been arrested and brought in for trial.

9*

be actively kept up in such of our districts as
border upon them, and the local magistrates continue to give the Oude authorities their cordial
support and co-operation; nor have I much doubt
of ultimate success in Western Malwa,* Guzerat,
Rajpootana, and the Delhi territories.   Great progress has been made in the extensive territories of
the Nizam, south of the Nerbudda, by' Captain
Reynolds, under the auspices of the Resident,
Colonel Stewart; and as the Bombay Government-
and local authorities in the conterminous districts
of that Presidency have manifested the most
anxious wish to co-operate, those of Madras will
probably do the same, and we shall then have a
fair prospect of ultimate success throughout the
countries south of the Nerbudda.
    Something has been done in Behar by Mr.
Peploe Smith, a very active and intelligent magistrate, and by Mr. C. W. Smith and others,
and what has been done may lead to more; but
the provinces of Behar, Bengal, and Orissa, are
those in which my hopes of final success are
perhaps least sanguine.   The river Thugs of
Bengal, who reside chiefly in the district of
Burdwan, on the banks of the Hooghly, will defy
all our efforts unless some special measure be
adopted by the government for the suppression of
their system, and we have, to promote its success,
a combination of circumstances almost too favourable to be hoped for.   They are supposed to be
between two and three hundred, and to employ
about twenty boats, which pass up and down the
Ganges during the months of November, Decem-

---

* Indeed Major Borthwick's great success in Western Malwa
has left but little to accomplish in that quarter.

ber, January, and February. Each boat is provided with a crew of about fourteen persons, all
Thugs, but employed in different capacities. Some
are employed in pulling the boat along by a rope,
and appear like the dandies or rowers and pullers
of ordinary boats; some as *Sothas,* or inveiglers,
follow the boats along the roads that run parallel
with the river, and by various arts prevail upon
travellers to embark as passengers on board their
boats, where they find many Thugs well dressed
and of the most respectable appearance, pretending
to be going on or returning from a pilgrimage to
the holy places of Guya, Benares, Allahabad, &c.
These are the stranglers and their assistants, who
on a signal given by the man at the helm on deck
(*Bykureea*), strangle the travellers, break their
back bones and push them out of a window in the
side into the river. Each boat has one of these
windows on each side, and they are thrust out of
that facing the river.

Several boats belonging to the same association
follow each other at the distance of from four to
six miles, and when the travellers show any signs
of disliking or distrusting the inveigler of one, or
any disinclination to embark at the ghat where his
boat is to be found, the inveigler of the one in
advance learns it by signs from the other, as he
and the travellers overtake him. The new inveigler gets into conversation with the travellers, and
pretends to dislike the appearance of the first, who
in his turn, pretends to be afraid of the new one,
and lags behind, while the new man and the travellers congratulate each other on having shaken
off so suspicious a character. These men never
shed blood, and if any drop touch them they must
return and offer sacrifices of some kind or other.

They never keep any article that can lead to suspicion, as their boats are constantly liable to be searched by the custom-house officers. Nothing I believe could tempt them to murder a woman. This class contains Mahommuduns and Hindoos of all casts, and they go up the river Ganges as far as Benares, and sometimes even as far as Cawnpore, it is said ; and they carry on their depredations as well going down as coming up the river. The Lodahas, Moteeas, and Jumaldehee Thugs, who reside in Behar and Bengal, are all acquainted with them, as the principal scene of their operations is along the banks of the Ganges and other large rivers into which they throw the bodies of their victims. Their resting places or Thapas, are almost always upon the banks of these rivers, where the large and most frequented roads approach nearest to them ; and there they remain for a long time together, destroying such travellers as they can persuade to spend the night with them. When they fall in with the boats, and see a chance of a good prize, some of the members of their gang go on board and assist in the murder; and the whole gang share equally with that of the boatmen in the spoil.

Our present plan of operations for the suppression of this system commenced with the arrest of a large gang from Hindoostan on its return from an expedition into the Duckun by Captain, now Major Borthwick, Political Agent at Mahidpore ;*

* Major Borthwick, on the 7th of November, 1831, accompanied by Captain McMahon and a party of two hundred of the Jowra Cavalry Contingent, made a night march of thirty miles, and arrested an entire gang of forty-six of these murderers, with property to the value of about twelve thousand rupees, which they had brought home from a recent expedition in which they had

and that of another by me in Bhopaul in the beginning of 1830.* These arrests were attended by a combination of circumstances so fortunate, that a man might consider them as providential without exposing himself to the charge of superstition. The feelings of every one whose feelings were of any importance to the cause, from the Governor General Lord Wm. Bentinck and Vice President in Council, Sir Charles Metcalfe, to the humblest individual, seemed to be deeply and simultaneously interested in promoting its success. Colonel Stewart, who was at the time the representative of the government at the Court of Indore, tried the gang arrested by Captain Borthwick, under instructions from the supreme government; and he long afterwards declared " that he considered the share " he had in bringing these men to punishment as " by far the most useful .part of his public life," though few men in India have, I believe, had a more useful ' career. Mr. Smith, who was the Governor General's representative in the Saugor

murdered a great many persons. His exertions in the cause have been unwearied, and eminently successful, and the gangs of Western Malwa have been almost entirely extirpated by his means.

* A gang of one hundred and five was arrested by Mr. Molony as they were crossing the valley of the Nerbudda from the Duckun after the Lucknadown murders in 1823. The bodies of the murdered people were pointed out and taken up at the time, but the death of Mr. Molony and other circumstances deferred the trial till 1830. Another large gang was arrested on its return from the Duckun over the same road by Captain Wardlow in 1826, and sent to Mr. C. Fraser at Jubulpore. He had the bodies of a great number of people whom they had murdered along the road disinterred; and having committed the case for trial to Mr. Wilder, then Agent of the Governor General at Jubulpore, they were all convicted, and punished. Another was seized by Major Henley at Bhopaul; and these several seizures may be considered as having laid the foundation of the subsequent proceedings in having furnished such numerous sources of information.

and Nerbudda Territories, has felt the same with
regard to his share in bringing the other gangs to
punishment.

The government observed upon the trial of the
Mahidpore gang—

" These murders having been perpetrated in
" territories belonging to various native chiefs, and
" the perpetrators being inhabitants of various dis-
" tricts belonging to different authorities, there is
" no chief in particular, to whom we could deliver
" them for punishment, as their sovereign, or as the
" prince of the territory in which the crime had
" been committed."

" The hand of these inhuman monsters' being
" against every one, and there being no country
" within the range of their annual excursions from
" Bundelcund to Guzerat in which they have not
" committed murder, it appears to His Lordship in
" Council, that they may be considered like pirates,
" to be placed without the pale of social law, and
" be subjected to condign punishment by whatever
" authority they may be seized and convicted."*

It is a principle of the law of nations, recognized
I believe by every civilized people, that assassins
by profession shall find in no country a sanctuary,
but shall every where be delivered up to the
Sovereign who reclaims them, and in whose
dominions they have perpetrated their crimes ; and
as the crimes of these assassins are never confined
to the country in which they reside, and as every
country in India must now be considered as under

* See Mr. Secretary Swinton's letter to Colonel Stewart of the
23d October, 1829. To few men is the success which has attended
these operations more attributable than to Mr. George Swinton,
who was then Chief Secretary to Government and is now in
Europe.

the protection of the supreme government in some relation or other, that government very properly undertook the duty which seemed to be imposed upon it by the laws of humanity and of nations, and determined to reclaim them from every state in which they might seek shelter.*

Unhappily there are in India few native chiefs who have any great feelings of sympathy even with the inhabitants of their own territories beyond their own family or clan, or any particular desire to protect them from the robber or the assassin ; and no instance can I believe be found of one extending his sympathies or his charities to the people of any other territory. They have, however, all a feeling of strong pride in claiming for their own territory the privilege of a sanctuary for the robbers and assassins of all other territories; while their public officers of every description and landholders of every degree convert this privilege, when conceded to their chiefs, into a source of revenue for themselves.

* " Although the justice of each nation ought in general to be
" confined to the punishment of crimes committed in its own terri-
" tories, we ought to except from this rule those villains, who by
" the nature and habitual frequency of their crimes violate all
" public security, and declare themselves the enemies of the human
" race. Poisoners, assassins, and incendiaries by profession,
" may be exterminated wherever they are seized : for they attack
" and injure all nations, by trampling under foot the foundations
" of their common safety. Thus pirates are sent to the gibbet by
" the first into whose hands they fall. If the sovereign of the
" country where crimes of that nature have been committed,
" reclaims the perpetrators of them in order to bring them to
" punishment, they ought to be surrendered to him, as being the
" person who is principally interested in punishing them in an
" exemplary manner. And as it is proper to have criminals regu-
" larly convicted by a trial in due form of law, this is a second
" reason for delivering up malefactors of that class to the States
" where their crimes have been committed.— *Vattel's Law of
Nature and Nations, Book I. Chap.* 19.

From the time that our government assumed,
under the Marquis of Hastings, its true and digni-
fied position as the protector of the society of India
generally against the savage inroads of the Pin-
dary hordes, the native chiefs considered themselves
as standing, with regard to us, in a relation entirely new; and bound to obey our call for aid and
support in the suppression of any system prejudicial
to the general interest and welfare of the community. They all knew that this system of merciless
and indiscriminate assassination was still more
general than that of the Pindaries, that it was the
growth of ages, extending all over India, and
being founded in the faith of religious *ordinance*
and *dispensation*, had become so deeply rooted in
the soil, that nothing but the interposition, under
Providence, of the supreme government, and the
acquiescence, support and co-operation of all its
dependent chiefs, could possibly extirpate it. But,
as in the case of the Pindaries, many of these native
chiefs or their officers and landholders, nevertheless sacrificed with reluctance, the revenues they
were in the habit of deriving from these people,
and with still more the pride of being thought able
to afford to them that asylum which others were
obliged to deny, and consequently, the *reputation*
of being able to refuse with impunity an acquiescence which others were obliged to concede to
the supreme government; and such men availed
themselves with avidity of the indolence, or indifference of the European functionaries by whom
our government happened to be represented. Happily they have been very rare, and the obstacles
which they have caused very few; while the
instances of the cordial, zealous, and active co-

operation of such functionaries have been very numerous.*

But it must be admitted that this evil has prevailed in our own provinces as much as in native states; and if I were called upon to state any single cause which has operated more than any other to promote its extension, I should say it was the *illogical* application in practice of the maxim, " that it is better ten guilty men should *escape*, than " that one innocent man should *suffer*." It is no doubt better that ten guilty men should *escape* the *punishment of death*, and all the eternal consequences which may result from it, than that one innocent man should suffer *that punishment;* but it is not better that ten assassins by profession should escape, and be left freely and impudently to follow every where their murderous trade, than that one innocent man should *suffer the inconvenience of temporary restraint;* and wherever the maxim has been so understood and acted upon, the innocent have been necessarily punished for the guilty. In a country like India, abounding in associations of this kind, and with every facility they could desire to promote their success, and with little communication of thought or feeling between the governing

* In addition to the political functionaries already named, I should name as having given us their cordial support and valuable aid—The Honourable R. Cavindish as Resident at the Court of Gwalior ; Major Alves as Political Agent in Bhopaul, and Agent in Rajpootana ; Colonel Spiers as Acting Agent in Rajpootana and Political Agent at Neemuch ; Mr. Wilkinson, Political Agent in Bhopaul ; Captain Wade, Political Agent at Lodheeana ; Mr. Græme and Colonel Briggs, Residents at the Court of Nagpore ; Captains Robinson and Johnstone as Assistants and Officiating Residents at the Court of Holcar ; Mr. Williams and Colonel Balfour at Baroda ; Major Ross, Political Agent at Kota ; and, though last not least, Mr. Ainslie and Mr. Begbie, as Agents to the Governor General at Bundelcund.

and the governed, the necessity of prosecuting gang robbers and murderers with such a maxim so understood and acted upon, is often found to be a greater surce of evil to the families and village communities who have suffered, than the robbers and murderers themselves; for the probability is always in favour of the criminals being released, however notorious their character and ·guilt, to wreak their vengeance upon them at their leisure, after the innocent and the sufferers have been ruined by the loss of time and labour wasted in attendance upon the Courts to give unavailing evidence.

It is a maxim with these assassins, that " dead men tell no tales," and upon this maxim they invariably act. They permit no living witness to their crimes to escape, and therefore never attempt the murder of any party until they can feel secure of being able to murder the whole. .They will travel with a party of unsuspecting travellers for days, and even weeks together, eat with them, sleep with them, attend divine worship with them at the holy shrines on the road, and live with them in the closest terms of intimacy till they find time and place suitable for the murder of the whole. Having in the course of ages matured a system by which the attainment of any other direct evidence to their guilt is rendered almost impossible, they bind each other to secresy by the most sacred oaths that thei superstition can afford ; and ·such associations never desire from any government a clearer *license* to their merciless depredations than a copy of the rule, " that the testimony of any number of confessing " prisoners shall not be sufficient ground to autho- " rize the detention of their associates ;" for if the confessing prisoners escape the laws of the country, they are put to death by the laws of the association. To suppress associations of this kind in such a country and such a society as those of India, a departure from rules like these, however suitable to ordinary times and circumstances, and to a more advanced and a more rational system of society, becomes indispensably necessary; and as they have matured their system to deprive all governments of every other kind of direct evidence to their guilt but the testimony of their associates, it behoves all governments, in order to relieve society from so intolerable an evil, to mature another by which their testimonies shall be rendered effectual for their conviction, without endangering the safety of the innocent. This I hope has now been done, but it can never be rendered so perfect as not to depend in some measure upon the personal character of the officers entrusted with its superintendence. There is no duty which requires higher qualifications for its proper discharge; and if these qualifications be not considered a point of paramount importance in the nomination of officers to the department, government will certainly not do its duty to the society.

The trial of these people for murders perpetrated in the Hydrabad and Indore dominions, was with the consent of the Nizam and Holcar governments, made over to the British Residents at their respective Courts, but subject to the revision and final orders of the supreme government. That of those charged with murders perpetrated in the Oude territory, has, with the consent of the King, been made over to the Resident at that Court. The trial of those charged with murders perpetrated in any other territory, and beyond the limits of districts in which our regulations are in force, was made over to the Governor General's Agent in the Saugor and Nurbudda territories, who has since for the time been entrusted, for special reasons assigned by the Resident and approved by government, with the trial of those charged with the murders in the Hydrabad territories also.

Thugs charged with murders perpetrated in the districts where our regulations are in force, were to be made over for trial to the regular tribunals; but, with the sanction of government previously obtained in any particular case, the venue might be changed from the Court of any one district to that of another, or to that of the special Commissioner for the whole, Mr. Stockwell, then Commissioner of the Allahabad division, who consented to undertake that in addition to his other duties, and who conducted, in that capacity, the trial of one of our most interesting and important cases committed to him by Mr. Wilson.

When I first undertook the duty of superintending the operation for the arrest of these gangs, and of collecting the evidence for the cases in which they were to be committed for trial, the most laborious and painful that I have ever performed, I had the civil charge of the district of Jubulpore on the Nurbudda river. As that of Saugor was more central, and consequently more eligible, I was in January, 1831, transferred to the civil charge of that district during the absence of Mr. C. Fraser on sick leave to the hills. On his return in January 1832, he resumed charge of the revenue and civil duties, and left me the criminal, which I continued to discharge till January 1835, while Captain Low continued to officiate for me in the civil charge of the Jubulpore district. By the resolution of government of the 10th January, 1835, my headquarters were transferred back to Jubulpore; and having the general superintendence of all proceedings preliminary to trial over the whole field of our operations, which had now extended from Lahore to the Carnatic, I was relieved from every other charge.

In May 1832, Captain Reynolds was appointed to superintend our operations south of the Nurbudda. In September 1832, Mr. Wilson was appointed to superintend those between the Ganges and the Jumna; and in February 1833, Mr. McLeod was appointed to superintend those in Rajpootana, Malwa, and the Delhi territories; and three officers with higher qualifications, for the very delicate and responsible duty in their respective spheres of action could not, I believe, have been any where found.

On the 10th of January 1835, Lieutenant Briggs, a very active and intelligent officer, was appointed to succeed Mr. McLeod in Malwa and Rajpootana, and Lieutenant Elwall, an officer equally well qualified, was appointed to assist Captain Reynolds south of the Nurbudda; and Captain Paton, Assistant to the Resident at the Court of Lucknow, was withdrawn from the general duties of the Residency, that he might afford his valuable aid exclusively to this department in Oude.

In March 1831, a tuman or company of Nujeebs was added to the Jubulpore local police corps, exclusively for employment under me in this duty; and in April another company was added to the same corps for employment under Captain Reynolds, south of the Nurbudda. The officer commanding the Saugor Division, Brigadier General O'Halloran, anxious to afford his aid in promoting the success of an undertaking of so much impor-

tance to the society of India generally, and to the
native army in particular, had given me the services of a detachment, under the command of an
excellent native officer Rustum Khan, in Bundlecund; and Brigadier General Smith, since he
succeeded to the command, has been equally anxious to afford his aid on all proper occasions. In
July 1833, when our means had become inadequate
for the vast field over which our operations extended, Messieurs Wilson and McLeod were, under
instructions from government,* allowed by the
officers commanding the divisions in which they
were employed each a detachment of forty regular
sipahees under a native commissioned officer, and
twenty troopers from the corps of local horse under
a Dufadar.

Knowing how many of their comrades used
annually to be murdered by these assassins on their
way home to their families on furlough, the pursuit
after them is a duty which these regular sipahees
very cheerfully perform, and are indeed extremely
proud of; and as the knowledge which they acquire
in the course of its discharge of their mode of
inveigling and destroying travellers is. communi-
cated to all the men of their regiments when they
rejoin, their employment on this has been unquestionably and will continue to be of great advantage
to the whole native army.

Thus far our highest political functionaries have
afforded their aid in the arrest and the trial of these
criminals cheerfully and gratuitously. Colonel
Stewart, Mr. Wellesley, Mr. Martin and Mr. Bax
successively at Indore, Colonel Stewart again at

* 40 Sipahees under a native commissioned Officer ; 20 Sowars
under a Dufadar for each of those two gentlemen. See proceedings
of the Governor General in Council, 28th June, 1833.

Hydrabad, and Mr. F. C. Smith in the more laborious office of the Saugor and Norbudda Agency; and proud indeed, might any man feel, however exalted his station, to be able to contribute his aid to the great work of relieving a society of one hundred millions of his fellow creatures from an evil so great, and so calculated from its character, and that of the deluded people among whom it has fallen, to penetrate and poison every source of confidence and security between man and man.

Among the people of India almost every man is married as soon as he has attained the proper age, and his parents can afford the expenses of the marriage ceremonies. The younger sons of poor but respectable families seek employment in distant public establishments, civil or military, while their wives and children remain united with the family under the care of their father or their elder brother, and the ties of duty and affection between them and their parents are never broken or impaired by any length of absence, or any new interests or connexions. During their absence these sons subject themselves to all kinds of privations in order that they may be able to send home the largest possible share of their incomes; and derive their greatest happiness from the hope of returning occasionally and enjoying for short and distant intervals, the society of their families thus united and bound together by ties so amiable. If any die their widows and children still remain with the family, and are maintained by the survivors; and all "delight to honour" the widow who honours the memory of her deceased husband. It is upon such families, who are to be found in almost every town in India, that the evil of this system of assassination presses most heavily. If the absent members do not return at the time they are expected, others proceed in search of them; and since I undertook this duty, numbers have flocked to me to inquire after the fate of those whom they had long lost. Often in my court I have seen them listening with unobtrusive grief to a circumstantial detail of the murder of their parents, brothers or children from the mouths of these cold-blooded and merciless assassins, while the tears stole down their cheeks; and taking from my stores of recovered property some sad token in arms, dress, or ornaments, of the melancholy truth to take home to the widows and children of the murdered, who might otherwise doubt their tale of sorrow, and entertain some lingering but unavailing hope of their return.*

---

* In January, 1831, a small gang was arrested and brought in to me at Saugor. One of the approvers, in deposing to the identity of one, mentioned that he had then on him, unaltered, the vest which they had taken some time before from Purtapa, a man whom they had murdered with his friend at Gola pass, on their way from Indore to Bhopaul. I had it taken off and sent immediately by the letter dawk to the resident at Indore, Mr. Wellesley. He was absent, but Captain Johnstone, the assistant resident, made the requisite inquiries and sent me the result. The reader may find it interesting. In the early stage of our proceedings such occurrences were very common.

Indore, 2d *February*, 1831.

Humeerchund, merchant of Indore, being called into court, gives the following statement:

"On Sunday, the 10th of the month of Poos, Sumbut, 1886, " (20th December, 1829,) my brother Purtapa and my wife's " brother Sooklall, proceeded towards Sehore with a tattoo, on " which was loaded about 400 rupees worth of English Chintz, " Mushroo, &c. They also carried with them 105 Halee rupees " in cash; and about 95 rupees of gold and gold ornaments. Not " having received any intelligence of them for 25 days after their " departure, I became anxious about their safety and hired a man " to go to Sehore and make inquiries of my correspondents there. " I ascertained that they had never reached that place. About

Should it be thought necessary I may perhaps hereafter give a more connected history of the

" three months afterwards, my younger brother Hunsraj, went in " quest of information, and found traces of Purtapa and Sooklall, " having been murdered near the Gola pass, a short distance beyond " Tuppa.*

" *Question.*—Do you recollect the ungurka which your brother " Purtapa wore when he left Indore ?

" *Answer.*—Yes, it was made of Europe chintz and lined with . " blue cotton."

The ungurka sent by Captain Sleeman, which corresponded with the above description, was shown to the witness who immediately recognised it, and was so much affected as scarcely to be able to speak. He took hold of the twisted silk cords attached to the ungurka, and said he had himself purchased them for his brother.

Hunsraj, brother of the preceding witness, being called, deposes as follows :—

" I returned to Indore from Rutlam about three months after " my brother Purtapa was missing, and then proceeded towards " Sehore for the purpose of inquiring after his fate. I ascertained " that he and my relation Sooklall had stopped the first night after " leaving Indore at Akeypoor, and the second at Pceplia. I found " they had left Pceplia on the morning of the third day, but I " could trace them no further. In the course of my inquiries at " Tuppa, I was informed by a Bunya that the bodies of some " persons had been found about three months previously near the " Gola pass, about two coss to the eastward of the town. He said " that a boy, the son of a Chumar belonging to Tuppa, observed a " number of jackals and vultures near the pass, and had gone " there in expectation of finding some dead animal and getting its " skin. On reaching the spot, however, he found the bodies of " two men which had been buried under a heap of stones so imper- " fectly, that the wild beasts had afterwards dragged them out and " almost entirely devoured them. The boy gave notice to the " villagers, who went to the pass and buried the remains of the " bodies. On hearing this account, I went to the Gola pass in com- " pany with the Bunya who pointed out the spot where the bodies

---

* Tuppa, half way between Ashta and Rajpoogur, and a coss pucka this side of Amla. One going from Ashta descends the Ghat about a pucka coss before he reaches Tuppa.

system and of our operations for its suppression, but for the present I can only offer, in addition to the above observations, the almost literal translation of some conversations I have had with the approvers in revising the vocabulary of their peculiar dialect for the last time. These conversations were often carried on in the presence of different European gentlemen who happened to call in, and as they seemed to feel a good deal of interest in listening to them, I thought others might possibly feel the same in reading them if committed to paper; and from that time I, for several days, put down the conversations as they took place in the the present form.

W. H. Sleeman,
Genl. Supt. for the Suppression of Thug Asscciations.

Head-Quarters,
Jubulpore, 8th Sept. 1835. }

"had been found. A large stone which lay near the place had "some marks of blood upon it, and on removing it I found a shoe, "which I at once recognised as having belonged to my brother, "and I wept bitterly. I took the shoe to Indore where it was "identified by the family, and as we had no doubt that our rela- "tions had been murdered, we performed their funeral rites accord- "ing to the customs of our sect."

The ungarka sent by Captain Sleeman was shown to the witness, but he said it had been made up while he was at Rutlam, and that he had not seen it before.

(Signed)   P. Johnstone,
                Assist. to the Resident.

The lad who had on the vest was the son of Kaleean Sing, Jemadar of Thugs, and now approver. He got it in a present from his uncle Dureean, and rather than alter so pretty a garment, he ran the risk of wearing it till he was taken.

W. H. S.

DISCLOSURES

OF.

THUG INFORMERS, MADE IN CONVERSATIONS HELD WITH
THEM BY CAPTAIN SLEEMAN, WHILE PREPARING HIS
VOCABULARY OF THEIR LANGUAGE.

THE following conversations form the most curious and interesting portion of Captain Sleeman's book. The perfect frankness of the disclosures, the coolness with which the most atrocious villanies are confessed and justified by an appeal to their superstitions; and the coincidence of the stories of different informers with respect to facts and motives, form one of the most singular chapters in the history of the human character. The explanation of the peculiar Thug terms, which sometimes occur, will be found by referring to the Vocabulary in the Appendix.

Q.—Do you ever recollect any misfortune arising from going on when a hare crossed the road before you?

Nasir, of Singnapore.—Yes; when General Doveton commanded the troops at Jhalna we were advancing towards his camp; a hare crossed the road; we disregarded the omen, though the hare actually screamed in crossing, and went on. The very next day I, with seventeen of our gang, were seized; and it was with great difficulty and delay that we got our release. We had killed some people, belonging to the troops, but fortunately none of their property was found upon us.

Q.—And you think these signs are all mandates from the deity, and if properly attended to, no harm can befall you?

Nasir.—Certainly; no one doubts it; ask any body. How could Thugs have otherwise prospered? Have they not every where been protected as long as they have attended religiously to their rules?

Q.—But if there was such a deity as *Bhowanee,** and she were your patroness, how could she allow me and others to seize and punish so many Thugs?

Nasir.—I have a hundred times heard my father and other old and wise men say, when we had killed a sweeper and otherwise infringed their rules, that we should be some day punished for it; that the European rulers would be made the instruments to chastise us for our disregard of omens, and neglect of the rules laid down for our guidance.

Q.—And you really believe that *Bhowanee* sends these signs to warn you of your danger, and guide you to your booty?

Nasir.—Can we—can any body doubt it? Did she not in former days when our ancestors attended to rules, bury the bodies for us, and save us the trouble; and remove every sign by which we could be traced?

Q.—You have heard this from your fathers, who heard it from their fathers; but none of you have ever seen it, nor is it true?

Nasir.—It is true, quite true; and though we have not seen this, we have all of us seen the sacred

---

* Bhowanee or Davey, a female goddess, is the tutelary deity of the Thugs.

pick-axe spring in the morning from the well into which it had been thrown over night, and come to the hands of the man who carried it at his call: nay we have seen the pick-axes of different gangs all come up of themselves from the same well at the same time, and go to their several bearers.

Q.—Yes; and you have all seen the common jugglers, by sleights of hand, appear to turn pigeons into serpents, and serpents into rabbits, but all know that they do it by their skill, and not by the aid of any goddess. The man who carries your pick-axe is selected for his skill, and gains extra emoluments and distinction; and no doubt can, in the same manner, make it appear that the axe comes out of itself when he draws it out by his sleight of hand.

Nasir.—With great energy—" What! shall not a hundred generations of Thugs be able to distinguish the tricks of man from the miracles of God? Is there not the difference of heaven and earth between them? Is not one a mere trick, and the other a miracle, witnessed by hundreds assembled at the same time?"

Q.—Sahib Khan, you are more sober than Nasir, have you ever seen it?

Sahib Khan.—On one expedition only.

Q.—Who were the pick-axe bearers?

Sahib.—They were Imam Khan and his brother.

Q.—From what country?

Sahib.—From Arcot. I was obliged to fly from Telingana when Major Parker and Captain Sheriff made their inroad upon us (Gurdee) and I went and joined the Arcot gangs. During a whole expedition that I made with them, Imam Khan and his brother carried the pick-axe, and I heard them repeatedly in the morning call them from the well into which they had thrown them over night, and saw the pick-axes come of themselves from the well, and fall into their aprons, which they held open *thus* :—Here he described the mode.

Q.—And you never saw any of your own gangs do this?

Sahib.—Never; I have Thugged for twenty years and never saw it.

Q.—How do you account for this?

Sahib.—Merely by supposing that they attend more to omens and regulations than we do. Among us it is a rule never to kill women; but if a rich old woman is found, the gang sometimes gets a man to strangle her by giving him an extra share of the booty, and inducing him to take the responsibility upon himself. We have sometimes killed other probibited people, particularly those of low cast, whom we ought not even to have touched.

Q.—You are from the Delhi clans?

Sahib.—Yes, I am of the Bursote clan, and my family went to the Dunkun, three generations ago.

Q.—Do you think the Arcot and Carnatic gangs are also from the Delhi clans?

Sahib.—We suppose that all Thugs originated by descent or initiation from the Delhi clans: but I think we are wrong. I became intimate with the Arcot gangs; and some of them, about seven years ago, after my return, came and settled in Telingana, between Hydrabad and Masulipatam, where they still carry on their trade of Thuggee; but they will never intermarry with our families—saying that we once *drove bullocks and were itinerant tradesmen*, and consequently of lower cast. They trace back the trade of Thuggee in their families to more generations than we can, and they are more skilful and observant of rules and omens than we are ; and I, therefore, think that they are neither descended from the Delhi stock, nor were ever disciples of theirs.

Q.—Do you think there is any truth in their assertion that your ancestors drove bullocks?

Sahib.—I think there is. We have some usages and traditions that seem to imply that our ancestors kept bullocks, and traded ; but how I know not.

Here a Brahman Thug, of one of the most ancient Thug families, interposed, and declared that he had seen the funeral rites of Musulman Thugs, and that the women who brought the water there chanted all the occupations of the ancestors of the deceased, which demonstrated that they were originally descended from gangs of wandering *Khunjurs*, or vagrant Musulmans, who followed armies and lived in the suburbs of cities, and in the wild wastes, and that their pretensions to higher descent was all nonsense. Several Musulman Thugs protested sturdily against this, but the arguments were too strong against them, and after a time the dialogue was resumed.

Q.—What do you think, *Sahib Khan*, am I right in thinking that we shall suppress Thuggee, or is *Nasir* right in thinking we shall not?

Sahib.—There have been several gurdies (inroads,) upon Thuggee, but they have ended in nothing but the punishment of a few ; and, as *Nasir* says, we have heard our fathers and sages predict these things as punishments for our transgression of prescribed rules; but none of them ever said that Thuggee would be done away with. This seems a greater and more general gurdie than any, and I know not what to think.

Q.—But tell me freely ; do you think we shall annihilate it?

Sahib.—How can the hands of man do away with the works of God.

Q.—You are a Musulman?

Sahib.—Yes, and the greater part of the Thugs of the south are Musulmans.

Q.—And you still marry; inherit; pray; eat and drink according to the Koran; and your paradise is to be the paradise promised by Mahommud?

Sahib.—Yes, all, all.

Q.—Has *Bhowanee* been any where named in the Koran?

Sahib.—No where.

Here a musulman Thug from Hindustan interposed, and said, he thought *Bhowanee* and *Fatima*, the daughter of Mahommud, and wife of *Alee*, were one and the same person; and that it was *Fatima* who invented the use of the *roomal* to strangle the great demon *Rukut-beej-dana;* which led to a discussion between him and some of my Musulman native officers, who did not like to find the amiable *Fatima* made a goddess of Thuggee—An " Iphigenia in Tauris." The Thug was a sturdy *wrangler*, and in the estimation of his associate Thugs had, I think, the best of the argument.

Q.—Then has *Bhowanee* any thing to do with your paradise?

Sahib.—Nothing.

Q.—She has no influence upon your future state?

Sahib.—None.

Q.—Does Mahommud, your prophet, any where sanction crimes like yours; the murder in cold blood of your fellow creatures for the sake of their money?

Sahib.—No.

Q.—Does he not say that such crimes will be punished by God in the next world?

Sahib.—Yes.

Q.—Then do you never feel any dread of punishment hereafter?

Sahib.—Never; we never murder unless the omens are favourable; and we consider favourable omens as the mandates of the deity.

Q.—What deity?

Sahib.—*Bhowanee.*

Q.—But *Bhowanee*, you say, has no influence upon the welfare or otherwise, of your soul hereafter?

Sahib.—None, we believe; but she influences our fates in this world, and what she orders in this world, we believe, that God will not punish in the next.

Q.—And you believe that if you were to murder without the observance of the omens and regulations, you would be punished both in this world and the next like other men?

Sahib.—Certainly; no man's family ever survives a murder: it becomes extinct. A Thug who murders in this way loses the children he has, and is never blessed with more.

Q.—In the same manner as if a Thug had murdered a Thug?

Sahib.—Precisely; he cannot escape punishment.

Q.—And when you observe the omens and rules, you neither feel a dread of punishment here nor hereafter?

Sahib.—Never.

Q.—And do you never feel sympathy for the persons murdered—Never pity or compunction?

Sahib.—Never.

11*

Q.—How can you murder old men and young children without some emotion of pity—calmly and deliberately, as they sit with you and converse with you,—and tell you of their private affairs, of their hopes and fears, and of the wives and children, they are going to meet after years of absence, toil and suffering?

A.—From the time the omens have been favourable, we consider them as victims thrown into our hands by the deity to be killed; and that we are the mere instruments in her hands to destroy them : that if we do not kill them, she will never be again propitious to us, and we and our families will be involved in misery and want.

Q.—And you can sleep as soundly by the bodies or over the graves of those you have murdered, and eat your meals with as much appetite as ever?

Sahib.—Just the same; we sleep and eat just the same unless we are afraid of being discovered.

Q.—And when you see or hear a bad omen, you think it is the order of the deity not to kill the travellers you have with you or are in pursuit of?

Sahib.—Yes; it is the order not. to kill them, and we dare not disobey.

Q.—Do your wives never reproach you with your deeds?

Sahib.—In the south we never tell our wives what we do lest they should disclose our secrets.

Q.—And if you told them would they not reproach you?

Sahib.—Some would, and some, like those of other Thugs who do tell them, would quietly acquiesce.

Q.—And be as affectionate and dutiful as the wives of other men?

Sahib.—The fidelity of the wives of Thugs is proverbial throughout India.

Q.—That is among Thugs?

Sahib.—Yes.

Q.—And the fear of the *roomal* (*Pehloo*) operates a little to produce this?

Sahib.—Perhaps a little, but there have been very few instances of women killed for infidelity among us.

Q.—And your children too reverence their Thug fathers like other sons, even after they have become acquainted with their trade?

Sahib.—The same : we love them and they love us the same.

Q.—At what age do you initiate them?

Sahib.—I was initiated by my father when I was only thirteen years of age.

Q.—Have you any rule as to the age?

Sahib.—None ; a father is sometimes avaricious, and takes his son out very young, merely to get his share of the booty ; for the youngest boy gets as much in his share as the oldest man : but generally a father is anxious to have his son in the rank of the. *Burkas* as soon as possible ; he does not like to have him considered a *Kuboola* after he has attained the age of puberty.

Q.—How soon do you let them see your operations?

Sahib.—The first expedition they neither see nor hear any thing of murder. They know not our trade, they get presents, purchased out of their share, and become fond of the wandering life, as they are always mounted upon ponies. Before the end of the journey they know that we rob. The next expedition they suspect that we commit murder, and some of them even know it; and in the third expedition they see all.

Q.—Do they not become frightened?.

Sahib.—Not after the second or third expedition.

Feringeea.—About twelve years ago my cousin Aman Subahdar took out with us my cousin Kurhora, brother of Omrow approver, a lad of fourteen, for the first time. He was mounted upon a pretty pony, and Hursooka, an adopted son of 'Aman's was appointed to take charge of the boy.

We fell in with five Sikhs, and when we set out before daylight in the morning, Hursooka, who had been already on three expeditions, was ordered to take the bridle and keep the boy in the rear out of sight and hearing. The boy became alarmed, and impatient, got away from Hursooka, and galloped up at the instant the *J,hirnee,* or signal for murder was given. He heard the screams of the men, and saw them all strangled. He was seized with a trembling, and fell from his pony; he became immediately delirious, was dreadfully alarmed at the sight of the turbans of the murdered men, and when any one touched or spoke to him; talked about the murders and screamed exactly like a boy talks in his sleep, and trembled violently if any one spoke to him or touched him. We could not get him on, and after burying the bodies, Aman and I, and a few others, sat by him while the gang went on : we were very fond of him, and tried all we could to tranquillize him, but he never recovered his senses, and before evening he died. I have seen many instances of feelings greatly shocked at the sight of the first murder, but never one so strong as this. Kurhora was a very fine boy, and Hursooka took his death much to heart, and turned

Byragee ; he is now at some temple on the bank of the Nerbudda river.

Q.—Was not Jhurhoo, who was taken with your gang after the Bhilsa murders, and hung at Jubulpore, a brother of his ?

Feringeea.—Yes, poor Jhurhoo ! you ought not to have hung him ; he never strangled or assisted in strangling any man ! ! Here the tears ran down over Feringeea's face. Strange as it may seem, I have never heard him speak of his young cousin Jhurhoo's fate without weeping, and yet all the males of his family have been Thugs for ten generations. Another brother of this Jhurhoo, is a very noted Thug leader, still at large—Phoolsa.

Q.—Do you in the Duckun send any offerings to the Brahmans of the temple of *Davey?*

Feringeea.—Never ; we neither make offerings to her temples, nor do we ever consult any of her priests or those of any other temples. Our sages alone are consulted, and they consult omens alone as their guides.

Q.—Have they any written treatises on augury ?

Feringeea.—None ; they never consult books ; they learn all from tradition and experience.

Q.—But you worship at *Davey's* temples?

Feringeea.—Yes, of course, all men worship at her temple.

Q.—No.—We *Sahib loge* never do.

Feringeea.—I mean all Hindoos and Musulmans. Here my Mahommudun officers again interposed, and declared that they never did ; that it was only the very lowest order of Musulmans that did. But, unfortunately, these keen observers of passing events had seen the wives of some very respectable Musulmans at Jubulpore, during the time that the small pox was raging, take their children to her temples and prostrate them before the images of the Goddess of Destruction. The officers admitted this to be sometimes the case, but pretended that it was unknown to their husbands.

Sahib Khan and *Nasir.*—In the Duckun the greatest Nawabs and officers of state worship at the temples, and prostrate themselves and their children before the image of the Goddess when the small pox or the cholera morbus rages. We have ourselves seen them do it often.

Q.—And do they believe you Thugs to be under her special protection?

Sahib and *Nasir.*—Some of them do, and though they often try to dissuade us from our trade, they are afraid to punish us. Bura Sahib Jemadar, of Madura, had several hundred followers, and used to make valuable presents to Nawab Dollee Khan who knew how he got them, and offered him a high post with rent-free lands if he would leave off the trade. He would not.

Q.—What became of him at last?

Sahib and *Nasir.*—There was a great Decoit leader of the same name who had been committing great ravages, and orders were sent by the Nawab to the local officers to blow him away from a gun as soon as they could seize him. They seized Sahib Khan Thug, and blew him away by mistake before the Nawab got information of the arrest. In a few hours after his death a message came from the Nawab to say that he feared there might be a mistake, and when he heard that Sahib Khan Thug had been blown away, he was much grieved, but said that God must have ordained it, and the fault was not his.

Q.—Has he any sons?

Sahib and *Nasir.*—Yes. He has two; Ameen

Sahib, forty-five years of age, who has a gang of thirty Thugs, and Rajee Khan, forty years of age, who has a gang of ten Thugs, all from among their relations and connexions; and they act together and live in Omurda, Taalluk Afzulpore, in the Hyderabad territories.

Q.—What made your friends desert their old abodes in Arcot?

Sahib and *Nasir.*—Some magistrate got hold of some Thugs who turned informers, and gave them a good deal of annoyance.

Q.—Have they returned?

Sahib and *Nasir.*—Some. of them have gone back, and a great many who had not been molested remained there till the annoyance was over.

Q.—What leaders came away?

Sahib and *Nasir.*—Sheikh Amed who is considered the most able leader of his day. He has sixty fully initiated Thugs (*Borkas*) who pretend to be recruits for regiments. He is thoroughly acquainted with the drill of the Company's regiments and their military terms, and can speak English.

Q.—How do you know? You do not understand English.

Sahib and *Nasir.*—He can make the gentlemen and those who speak English understand when he speaks a language we do not understand, and he tells us this is English. Other Thug leaders generally display their wealth in an ostentatious appearance that betrays them. Sheikh Amed is sixty years of age, and will go about for months cooking his own food, walking and living like the poorest man, while he can command the services of a hundred men.

Q.—Who are the others?

Sahib and *Nasir.*—Osman Khan, who has about

thirty *Borkas*, or fully initiated and able Thugs. He is, fifty years of age.

Husun Khan, who has twenty-five *Burkas*, and is fifty-five years of age.

Sahib Khan of Lodeekar, who has thirty *Borkas*, and is forty-five years of age.

Tipoo Jemadar, brother of Sahib Khan, who has ten *Borkas*, and is about forty years of age.

Hoseyn Khan, the nephew of Husun Khan, who has about six *Borkas*, and is thirty-five years of age.

Noor Khan, who has ten, and is about forty : all these leaders came to Telingana from the Carnatic, about the same time, and settled near Nulganda, about fifty cose from Hyderabad, on the road to Masulapatam, and they operate on the roads leading to the seaports.

Q.—You consider that a *Borka* is capable of forming a gang in any part of India to which he may be obliged to fly ?

Sahib and *Nasir.*—Certainly; in any part that we have seen of it.

Q.—Do you know any instance of it ?

Sahib and *Nasir.*—A great number. Mudee Khan was from the old Sindouse stock, and was obliged to emigrate after the attack upon that place. Many years afterwards we met him in the Duckun, and he had then a gang of fifty Thugs of all casts and descriptions. I asked him who they were; he told me that they were weavers, braziers, bracelet-makers, and all kinds of ragamuffins, whom he had scraped together about his new abode on the banks of the Herun and Nurbudda rivers, in the districts of Jebulpore and Nursingpore. He was a Musulman, and so were Lal Khan, Kalee Khan, who formed gangs after the Sindouse dispersion along the same rivers.

Q.—Did they find the same patrons among the landholders and other heads of villages ?

Sahib and *Nasir.*—They every where made friends by the same means; and without patrons they could not have thrived. They were obliged of course to give them a liberal share of the booty.

Q.—But these men have all been punished, which does not indicate the protection of *Davey* ?

Sahib and *Nasir.*—It indicates the danger of scraping together such a set of fellows for Thuggee. They killed all people indiscriminately, women and men, of all casts and professions, and knew so little about omens that they entered upon their expeditions and killed people, in spite of such as the most ignorant ought to have known were prohibitive. They were punished in consequence, as we all knew that they would be ; and we always used to think it dangerous to be associated with them for even a few days. Ask many of them who are now here,—Kureem Khan, Sheikh Kureem, Rumzanee and others, whether this is not true, and whether they ever let go even a sweeper if he appeared to have a rupee about him !

Q.—And you think that if they had been well instructed in the signs and rules, and attended to them, they would have thrived ?

Sahib and *Nasir.*—Undoubtedly ; so should we all.

Q.—You think that a *Kuboola* or tyro could not any where form a gang of Thugs of himself ?

Sahib and *Nasir.*—Never ; he could know nothing of our rules of augury, or proceedings , and how could he possibly succeed? Does not all our success depend upon knowing and observing omens and rules?

Q.—It would therefore never be very dangerous to release such a man as a *Kuboola?*

Sahib and *Nasir.*—Never; unless he could join men better instructed than himself. Every one must be convinced that it is by knowing and attending to omens and rules that Thuggee has thrived:

Q.—I am not convinced, nor are any of the *native officers* present; on the contrary, we do all we can to put down what you call an institution of the deity, and without dreading at all the effects of her resentment?

Sahib and *Nasir.*—They may say so, but they all know that no man's family can survive a murder committed in any other way; and yet Thugs have thrived through a long series of generations. We have all children like other men, and we are never visited with any extraordinary affliction.

Q.—Tell me frankly which oath, now while you are in custody, you who are Musulmans deem the strongest,—that upon the Koran or that upon the pick-axe?

Sahib and *Nasir.*—If we could be allowed to consecrate the pick-axe in the prescribed form, neither the Koran nor and thing else on earth could be so binding; but without consecration it would be of no avail.

Q.—Do you not sometimes make up a piece of cloth in the jail in the form of a pick-axe, and swear upon it?

Sahib and *Nasir.*—We have heard that the Hindustan Thugs do, but we have never seen it.

Q.—Do you think it answers?

Sahib and *Nasir.*—It may with proper conse-

cration ceremonies, but we have never tried it.
Even *mud* made into the same form and consecrated would do.   If any man swears to a falsehood upon a pick-axe, properly consecrated, we
will consent to be hung if he survives the time
appointed; appoint one, two or three days when he
swears, and we pledge ourselves that he does not
live a moment beyond the time; he will die a horrid death; his head will turn round, his face
towards the back, and he will writhe in tortures till
he dies.

Q.—And all this you have seen?

Sahib and *Nasir.*—Yes, we have all seen it.

Q.—Above the Norbudda, chiefs have never had
the same dread of punishing Thugs as below it;
have they?

Feringeea.—They had formerly, and have still in
many parts.

Q.— Why should they fear ; have there been any
instances of suffering from it ?

Feringeea.—A great many.   Was not Nanha,
the Raja of Jhalone, made leprous by *Davey* for
putting to death Bodhoo and his brother Khumolee,
two of the most noted Thugs of their day.   He
had them trampled under the feet of elephants, but
the leprosy broke out upon his body the very next
day.

Q.—Did he believe that this punishment was
inflicted by *Davey* for putting them to death.

Dorgha Musulman.—He was quite sensible of
it.

Q.—Did he do any thing to appease her ?

Dorgha.—Every thing.   Bodhoo had began à
well in Jhalone; the Raja built it up in a magnificent style; he had a chubootra (tomb) raised to
their name, fed Brahmuns, and consecrated it, had

worship instituted upon it, but all in vain; the disease was incurable, and the Raja died in a few months a miserable death. The tomb and well are both kept up and visited by hundreds to this day, and no one doubts that the Raja was punished for putting these two Thugs to death.

Q.—But Bodhoo had his nose and hands cut off before, and could have been no favourite of *Davey's?*

Feringeea.—But he was a Thug of great repute; for sagacity we have never seen his equal; people who had been robbed used to go to him as an oracle.

Q.—But he had turned informer, and was sent to Jhalone by Mr. Stockwell to arrest his associates.

Dorgha.—He went to Mr. Stockwell in a passion; his heart was not fully turned away from us then.

Q.—Have you any other instances?

Inaent.—Hundreds! When Madhajee Scindheea caused seventy Thugs to be executed at Muthura, was he not warned in a dream by *Davey* that he should release them? and did he not the very day after their execution begin to spit blood? and did he not die within three months?

Feringeea.—When Dureear the Rathore, and Komere and Patore, the Kuchwaha Rajpoots, Zumeendars, arrested eighty of the Thugs who had settled at Nodha after the murder of Lieut. Monsell, they had many warnings to let them go; but they persisted and kept them till some thirty died. They collected fourteen thousand rupees at the rate of one hundred and twenty-five rupees from every Thug. What became of their families? Have they not all perished? They have not a child left. Rae Sing Havildar, the Gwalior Subah of Nodha, took the money, but that very day his only son and the best horse in his stable died, and he was himself taken ill and died soon after a miserable death.

Nasir.—Ah *Davey* took care of you then, and why? Was it not because you were more attentive to her orders?

Zolfukar.—Yes; we had then some regard for *religion.* We have lost it since. All kinds of men have been made Thugs, and all classes of people murdered, without distinction, and little attention has been paid to omens. How after this could we expect to escape?

Nasir.—Be assured that *Davey* never forsook us till we neglected her.

Q.—Do you know of any instance of her punishing a man for annoying Thugs in the Duckun?

Sahib Khan.—A great many. The Raja of Kundul, some ninety cose east from Hydrabad, arrested all the Thugs in his Raj for some murders they had committed. For three successive nights the voice of *Davey* was heard from the top of every temple in the capital, warning the Raja to release them. The whole town heard her, and urged the Raja to comply. He was obstinate, and the third night the bed on which he and his ranee were sleeping was taken up by *Davey* and dashed violently against the ground.

Q.—Were they killed?

Nasir.—They were not killed, but they were dreadfully bruised; and had they not released the Thugs, they would certainly have been killed the next night.

Q.—Were any of you present?

Sahib Khan.—Our fathers were, and we heard it from them. It occurred sixty years ago.

12*

Q.—And do you think that the chiefs have still the same dread of punishing Thugs in all parts of India ?

Sahib.—Certainly not in all parts; because in many they have been suffered to punish them with impunity on account of their neglect of rules and omens.

Morlee.—There is no fear now. They are every where seized and punished with impunity; there is no resisting your *Ikbal* (good fortune).

Dorgha.—The Company's *Ikbal* is such that before the sound of your drums, sorcerers, witches and demons take flight, and how can Thuggee stand.

Davey Deen.—Thuggee ! why it is gone ; there are not fifty Aseel Thugs, (Thugs of good birth) left between the Ganges and Jumna.

Chotee Brahman.—And not more than that number of all our old clans of Gwalior and Bundelcund ; but the Sooseas of Rajpootana have been untouched, and much is to be done about Delhie and Puteeala.

Q.—But Nasir and Sahib Khan think that it can never be suppressed in the Duckun ?

Nasir.—I think it never can.

Sahib Khan.—I do not say it never can. I say only that the country is very large ; that in every one of the five districts there are hundreds of Aseel Thugs, who are staunch to their oath, and attentive to their usages ; that the country is every where intersected by the jurisdiction of native chiefs who cannot be easily persuaded to assist.

Nasir.—Assist ! why when we go into their districts after a Thug we are every instant in danger of our lives. I got nearly killed with all the guard lately when close upon the heels of a gang, and when I complained to Captain Reynolds, he told me that we must consent to bear these drubbings on account of the Company, or I could be of no use to him in such a country as that!

Q.—And you think that all these obstacles are not to be overcome?

Nasir.—I think not.

Q.—That is, you think an institution formed by *Davey*, the Goddess, cannot be suppressed by the hand of man?

Nasir.—Certainly, I think so.

Q.—But you think that no man is killed by man's killing, " *admeeke marne se koee murta nuheen ;*" that all who are strangled are strangled, in effect, by God.

Nasir.—Certainly.

Q.—Then by whose killing have all the Thugs who have been hung at Saugor and Jubulpore been killed?

Nasir.—God's of course.

Q.—You think that we could never have caught and executed them but by the aid of God.

Nasir.—Certainly not.

Q.—Then you think so far we have been assisted by God in what we have done?

Nasir.—Yes.

Q.—And you are satisfied that we should not have ventured to do what we have done unless we were assured that our God was working with us, or rather that we were the mere instruments in his hands?

Nasir.—Yes, I am.

Q.—Then do you not think that we may go on with the same assurance till the work we have in hand is done; till in short, the system of Thuggee is suppressed?

Nasir.—God is almighty.

Q.—And there is but one God?

Nasir.—One God above all Gods.

Q.—And if that God above all Gods supports us, we shall succeed?

Nasir.—Certainly.

Q.—Then we are all satisfied that he is assisting us, and therefore hope to succeed even in the Duckun?

Nasir.—God only knows.

Sahib Khan.—If God assists, you will succeed; but the country is large and favourable, and the gangs are numerous and well organized.

Q.—So was the country we have already gone over. How many Thug leaders from Sindouse after Mr. Halhed and Mr. Stockwell's attacks came and settled in the Saugor and Nurbudda districts?

Shiekh Inayat.—My father Hinga Jemadar and his three sons, two of whom were hung at Saugor the year before last, came to Lowa, a village between Dhamonee and Khimlassa in Saugor; my younger brother Dhurum Khan was born after my father's death; his mother could not, and my wife nursed him. We were joined by Monowur Musulman, Niddee and Mungoa Brahmans, Lulloo and his sons.

Q.—And how many noted Thugs and the gangs they formed are still at large.

Sheikh Inayat.—Since I was taken in 1829, these have all been seized, and have been hung or transported or are now in jail. Two of my brothers have been hung. My youngest is now here. The men whom they made Thugs have also been taken, and there are only five or six that we know of. There are Bahadur Chabukaswur, Kuscea

Kirar, Bodhooa, son of another Bahadur: these are new Thugs; but they proved themselves good ones. There are Kadir and Poosoo, adopted sons of Imamee, the son of Mirja Musulman. These Thugs are at large in the district of Seonee or Nursingpore. We know of no others.

Q.—Do you think that if we persevere, we shall be able to do in the Duckun what we have done here, and in the Dooab?

Inaent.—No doubt.

Sahib Khan.—It will be a work of greater difficulty. Half or three-quarters of these gangs were Kuboolas. In the Duckun they are almost all composed entirely of *Burkas*—men well born, staunch and able; above all the men of Arcot.

Feringeea.—And the Hindoo Thugs of Talghat upon the Krishna river?

Sahib Khan.—Yes; they are extraordinary men.

Feringeea.—They have three painted lines on their foreheads extending up from a central point at the nose. I served with them once for two months.

Sahid Khan.—Yes; they have these lines.

Q.—But do not all Hindoos in that quarter wear the same marks?

Sahib Khan.—All Hindoos put them on occasionally, but they always wear them. They and the Arcot Thugs associate and act together; but they will never mix with us of Telingana.

Q.—What are they called?

Sahib Khan.—We call them the Talghat men. What they call themselves I know not.

Q.—Sahib Khan tells tells me that the Arcot men will not intermarry with the descendants from the old Delhi clans, because they think they were orig05ally of lower cast ?

Sahib Khan.—But we refuse our daughters to them as they refuse theirs to us; and they are in error when they suppose us of low origin.

Q.—Have you Hindoostan men any funeral ceremonies by which your origin can be learnt?

Inaent.—No funeral ceremonies; but, at marriages an old matron will sometimes repeat, as she throws down the *Toolsee,* " Here's to the spirits of those who once led bears, and monkeys; to those who drove bullocks, and marked with the godnee; and those who made baskets for the head."

Q.—And does not this indicate that your ancestors were Khunjurs, itinerant tradesmen, wandering with their herds and families about the country.

Sahib Khan.—By no means. It only indicates that our ancesters after their captivity at Delhi, were obliged to adopt these disguises to effect their escape. Some pretended to have dancing bears and monkeys; some to have herds of cattle, and to be wandering Khunjurs, (Gypies); but they were not really so; they were high cast Musulmans.

Dorgha.—Certainly. I have heard this often from our wise men.

Feringeea.—You may hear and say what you please, but your funeral and marriage ceremonies indicate that your ancestors were nothing more than Khunjurs and vagrants about the great city?

Inaent.—It is impossible to say whether they were really what is described in these ceremonies, or pretended to be so; that they performed these offices for a time is unquestionable, but I think they must have been assumed as disguises.

Feriugeea.—But those who emigrated direct from Delhi into remote parts of India, and did not rest at Agra, retain those professions up to the present day ; as the Moltanies.

Sahib Khan.—True ; but it is still as disguises to conceal their real profession of Thuggee.

Feringeea.—True, and under the same guise they practised their trade of Thuggee round Delhi before the captivity, and could never have had any other.

Sahib.—I pretend not to know when they put on the disguise, but I am sure it was a disguise ; and that they were never really leaders of bears and monkeys.

Q.—Have the Talghat men the same language and usages as you have ?

Sahib.—They have the same omens and language, and observe the same rules ; but we hear that they use the round instead of the oblong grave to bury their victims, the same as the Behar men. They call it the *Chukree;* the Behar men and others call it the *Gobba.*

Q. — You call yourselves Telingana Thugs. What do you understand by the term ?

Sahib.—The country extending from Nandair to Nulgonda, which is four stages from Hydrabad on the road to Musalapatam.

Q.—How many divisions do the Thugs count in the Duckun; that is, the country south of the Nurbudda ?

Sahib.—There are five districts ; 1, Telingana ; 2, Berar, extending from Nagpore to Nandair ; 3, The Duckun, extending from Mominabad, which is fifty cose from Hyderabad on the road to Poona, to the city of Poona : 4, The Kurnatic, extending

from Satara to Kurpakundole; 5, Arcot, extending
from Kurpakundole to Seetabuldee Ramesur.

Q.—And the Thugs of these several divisions
consider themselves as distinct?

Sahib.—All distinct, and called after their divisions as Telinganies, Arcoties, Kurnatekies, Duckunees, and Beraries.

Q.—Can you name the principal leaders now at
large in these divisions?

Sahib.—Yes, all except those who reside in
Arcot. The only leaders of that district that I
know are the men already named, who occasionally go back, and always keep up their connexions with their old associates.

Q.—How is it that you Hindostan Thugs kill
women with less scruple than the Duckun Thugs?

Feringeea.—To that we owe much of our misfortunes. It began with the murder of the Kalee
Bebee.

Q.—Who was the Kalee Bebee?

Dorgha.—I was not present, but have heard that
she was on her way from Elichpore to Hyderabad
with a gold chadur or sheet for the tomb of Dolla
Khan Nowab, the brother of Salabut Khan of
Hyderabad, who had died just before. Shumshere
Khan and Golab Khan strangled her I believe.

Q.—When was this?

Dorgha.—It was I believe about four years
before the Surtrook affair in which we murdered
the sixty persons at Chitterkote, among whom were
some women.*

Q.—In what year did that take place?

---

* This gang of Thugs must have travelled above one hundred
and sixty miles with these people before they put them to death,
and been in company with them about twelve days, on the most
friendly terms.

Dorgha.—I do not know ; but it was either the year before, or two years before the Surgooja expedition in which the Chuleesrooh affair took place (forty persons at one time) where women were again murdered.

Q.—Do you recollect the year ?

Kuleean Sing.—The Surgooja expedition took place the year that Mr. Jenkins went first from Banares to Nagpore as Resident, and the Chuleesrooh was one of the affairs. He had just arrived and was encamped near the Seetabuldee hill when our gang reached Nagpore.

Q.—Did any calamity befal you after the murder of the Kalee Bebee ? ·

Dorgha.—I think not.

Q.—And therefore you continued to kill them ?

Feringeea.—For five years no misfortune followed, and they continued to kill women ; but then the misfortunes of my family began.

Q.—What relation had you there ?

Feeringeea.—My father Purusram was one of the principal leaders, and the chadur they got was worth about three thousand rupees. It was cut up and divided, and my father brought home one fine slip. But the fifth year after this his misfortunes began ; our family was never happy ; not a year passed without his losing something, or being seized ; he was seized every year some where or other.

Ghasee Subahdar was another leader, and he suffered similar misfortunes, and his family became miserable. Look at our families ; see how they are annihilated ; all that survive are in prison except Phoolsa and Rambuksh.

Q.—And still you went on killing women in spite

of your conviction that your misfortunes arose from it ?

Dorgha.—Yes, it was our fate to do so.

Q.—And you are worse than the Duckun Thugs, for you murder handsome young women as well as the old and ugly?

Feringeea.—Not always. I and my cousin Aman Subahdar were with a gang of one hundred and fifty Thugs on an expedition through Rajpootana about thirteen years ago when we met a handmaid of the Peshwa, Bajee Row's, on her way from Poona to Cawnpore. We intended to kill her and her followers; but we found her very beautiful, and after having her and her party three days within our grasp, and knowing that they had a lakh and a half of rupees worth of property in jewels and other things with them, we let her and all her party go: we had talked to her and felt love towards her, for she was very beautiful.

Q.—And how came you to kill the Moghulanee. She also is said to have been very handsome?

Feringeea.—We none of us ventured near her palankeen. The Musulmans were the only men that approached her before the murder. Madar Buksh approver strangled her.

Q.—And you think killing women has been one of the chief causes of your misfortunes?

Feringeea.—Yes.

Q.—And of our success against you?

Kuleean Sing.—Yes; I and my gang were arrested after the murder of Newul Sing and his daughters at Biseynee in 1820.

Q.—But Newul Sing had lost an arm, and you before told me that you suffered because you there infringed a good old rule and murdered a maimed person?

Kuleean.—Yes; it was partly that; but was not the great gang seized by Mr. Molony after the murder of Monshee Bunda Alee and his wife and daughter at Lucknadown, three years after?

Q.—Who was that Bunda Alee. I have never been able to discover?

Kuleean.—He was the Monshee of General Doveton, who commanded at Jhalna, and he was going to his home in Hindustan to celebrate the marriage of that daughter. His wife and an infant daughter and six servants, besides the eldest daughter, were all strangled.

Q.—Was not this about the time that you and your party were arrrested, Nasir, for not attending to the omen of the hare?

Nasir.—When we were taken before general Doveton he was in Durbar, and there was a Moonshee called Bunda Alee present. He did not write down our statements, but he asked questions, and explained them to the general. Rangrow Brahman, his Kamdar, wrote them down. He took down all the stages we had made, the names of our villages, and could not find any discrepancies.

Q.—Who denounced you to the general?

Nasir.—There were two brothers going to cantonments with bullocks, one had gone on in advance, and the other we murdered. The man in advance came back for his brother, and seeing us one hundred and fifty Thugs, and not finding his brother, he suspected us of the murder. A large party of horse and foot came after us. All however made off but eighteen of the staunchest and of most respectable appearance, who remained to stop the pursuit. We pretended to have been going with our friends in search of service; and after a

long examination, Moonshee Bunda Alee urged the
improbability of so large a body of robbers coming
so far to murder one poor bullock driver. This
argument had weight; we were let go, and the
bullock man sent about his business.

Q.—Was this the same Bunda Alee who was
afterwards murdered, think you?

Nasir.—I do not know; I never saw him or
heard of him after that time.

Q.—How long ago was it?

Nasir.—About thirteen or fourteen years ago.

Q.—Had not the daughters of Newul Sing Jemedar prevented the gang from being imprisoned?

Kuleean.—Yes. Omrow Sing, Dufadar of Captain Nicholson's corps, was then on duty at Seonee.
The gang had brought on this family from Nagpore. They were Newul Sing, a Jemedar in the
Nizam's service, who had lost one arm, his brother
Hurbuns Sing, his two daughters, one thirteen and
the other eleven years of age, the two young men
who were to have been married to them on reaching home, Kuleean Sing and Aman, the brother of
the two girls, a boy about seven years of age, and
four servants. The house in which part of the
gang lodged at Dhoma took fire, and the greater
part of the gang were seized by the police, but
released at the urgent request of Newul Sing and
his daughters, who had become much attached to
Khimolee, the principal leader of the gang, and
some of the others. Omrow Sing Dufadar was a
relation of Newul Sing, and he assisted in getting
them released as he can now tell you. Had the
gang been then imprisoned and searched we must
have been discovered, as they had with them two
bags of silk taken from the three carriers on their
way from Nagpore to Jubulpore, whom we had

murdered in the great temple at Kamtee, where the cantonments now stand.

On reaching Jubulpore part of the gang went on. Adhartal and the rest lodged in the town with Newul Sing and his family. The merchants at Nagpore finding that their men with the silk had not reached Jubulpore, and hearing of our gang having passed, sent to their correspondents at Jubulpore, who got the Cotwal to search those who were lodged with Newul Sing. Hearing of the approach of the police, Khimolee again availed himself of the attachment of Newul Sing and his daughters, and the girls were made to sit each upon one of the two bags of silk while the police searched the place. Nothing was found, and the next day they set out and passed us at Adhartal, and five days after this they were all strangled at Biseynee.*

Q.—How did you not preserve the infant daughter of Bunda Alee Moonshee for adoption?

Chutter.—Ghubboo Khan strangled the mother while her infant was in her arms, and he determined to keep and adopt the child; but after the bodies had all been put into the grave, Dhunnee Khan urged him to kill the child also, or we should be seized on crossing the Nurbudda valley. He threw the child living in upon the dead bodies, and the grave was filled up over it.

Q.—And the child was buried alive?

* This gang accompanied Newul Sing and his family from near Nagpore through Seonee and Jubulpore to Biseynee, a distance of more than two hundred miles, and were with them about twenty days on the most intimate terms, before they put them all to death. The circumstance of Newul Sing's having lost an arm made them hesitate, and one gang separated from the main body before they reached Seonce rather than be present at his murder; and there seemed no chance of their being able to separate him from the rest.

13*

Chutter.—Yes. My brother Dulput and I were then mere children; we were seized in crossing the Nurbudda valley and never after released;–he is now dead and I am the only surviving son of Ghasee Subahdar.

Q.—How was that affair managed?

Chutter.—We fell in with the Moonshee and his family at Chupara, between Nagpore and Jubulpore; and they came on with us to Lucknadown, where we found that some companies of a native regiment under European officers, were expected the next morning. It was determined to put them all to death that evening, as the Moonshee seemed likely to keep with the companies. Our encampment was near the village, and the Moonshee's tent was pitched close to us. In the afternoon some of the officers' tents came on in advance, and were pitched on the other side, leaving us between them and the village. The Khulasies were all busily employed in pitching them, Noor Khan and his son Sadee Khan and a few others, went as soon as it became dark to the Moonshee's tent, and began to sing and play upon a Sitar, as they had been accustomed to do. During this time some of them took up the Moonshee's sword on pretence of wishing to look at it. His wife and children were inside listening to the music. The *Jhirnee,* or signal, was given, but at this moment the Moonshee saw his danger, called out murder, and attempted to rush through, but was seized and strangled. His wife hearing him, ran out with the infant in her arms, but was seized by Ghubboo Khan, who strangled her and took the infant. The other daughter was strangled in the tent. The saeses (grooms) were at the time cleaning their horses, and one of them seeing his danger, ran under the belly of his horse, and called out murder; but he was soon seized and strangled as well as all the rest.

Q.—How did not the Khalasies and others who were pitching their tent close by hear these calls for help?

Chutter.—As soon as the signal was given, those of the gangs who were idle began to play and sing as loud as they could; and two vicious horses were let loose and many ran after them calling out as loud as they could: so that the calls of the Moonshee and his party were drowned.

Q.—Do you Behar Thugs ever murder woman?

Moradun.—Never; we should not murder a woman if she had a lakh of rupees upon her.

Davey Deen.—Nor would the Dooab Thugs if she had two lakhs upon her.

Gopaul.—We have never been guilty of so great a crime in the Dooab or any part east of the Ganges and Jumna where I have been employed.

Q.—But you Bundelcund men murdered abundance?

Zolfukar.—Yes, and was not the greater part of Feringeea's and my gang seized after we had murdered the two women and little girl at Manora in 1830 near Saugor? And were we not ourselves both seized soon after? How could we survive things like that: our ancestors never did such things.

Feringea.—We had no sooner buried their bodies than I heard the *chirega,** and on leaving the ground we saw the *loharburhega;** these were signs that *Davey* was displeased, and we gave ourselves up for lost.

* See these words in the Vocabulary.

Q.—But some of the Dooab Thugs have murdered women in your expeditions on this side of the Jumna?

Davey Deen.—That was while they were in company with the Bundelcund and Saugor men.

Gopaul.—On the other side of the Jumna and Ganges, we never have done so.

Bhikka.—How could we do so? we do not even murder a person that has a cow with him.

Q.—Had not the fourteen persons murdered at Kotree a cow with them, and were there not women in the party, and all killed?

Chotee.—We were almost all Gwalior and Bundelcund and Saugor men in that gang, but we persuaded the party to sell us the cow at Shahpore; and we gave it to a Brahman at that place, and two or three days after they were all strangled at Kotree in Huttah. I pointed out the grave to Captain Crawford, and he took up the bodies.

Q.—And you could not have strangled them if they had not parted with the cow?

Chotee.—Certainly not; nor could we have made them part with her had we not pretended that we had vowed to make such an offering at Shahpore, and were very much in want of her.

Zolfukar.—Durgha and Feringeea have been confounding cases; I have heard of the Kalee Bebee it is true, but I was not at her murder; and yet I was at the taking of the sheets intended for the Nowab's tomb. Peer Mahommud was there, so also was Kadir, then a boy; and I have heard that he has still in his family one of the slips that fell to the share of his adopted father, the great Dhurum Khan.

Feringeea.—But was not my father Purusram in that affair?

Zolfukar.—He was, and so was Ghasee Subahdar, but no Kalee Bebee was killed in that affair. There were only three persons, and they were men. We got two sheets, one green and the other red.

Kadir.—I was a little boy and that was my first expedition, and I was mounted upon a pony. The piece of the chadar we gave to a priest, and it was taken and lodged in the Sangor Malkhana, and afterwards put up to auction I believe.

Zolfukur.—The two chadars were sent by Nowab Salabut Khan, the Elichpore Nowab, for the tomb of his brother Buhlole Khan, who had died at Hyderabad. Lalmun Musulman, and Khandee and his brother Nundun Brahmans, must know all about the Kalee Bebee; they are very old men.

Khandee and *Nundun,* brothers and Brahmans, one 83 and the other 85 years of age, being sent for, deny having been present at the murder, but say they knew of it, and of the dire effects of it to the Thug fraternity.

Lalmun.—Being sent for, age 90. I remember the murder of the Kalee Bebee well; I was at the time on an expedition to Barodah, and not present, but Punna must have been there. A dispute arose between the Musulmans and the Hindoos before and after the murder. The Musulmans insisted upon killing her, as he had four thousand rupees worth of property with her: the Hindoos would not agree. She was killed, and the Hindoos refused to take any part of the booty; they came to blows, but at last the Hindoos gave in, and consented to share in all but the clothes and ornaments which the women wore. Feringeea's father, Purusram Brahman, was there; so was Ghasee Subahdar, a Rajpoot; so was Himmut Brahman.

When they came home ·to Murnae, Rae Sing, Purusram's brother, refused to eat, drink or smoke with his brother till he had purged himself from this great sin; and he, Himmut, and Ghasee gave a feast that cost them a thousand rupees each. Four or five thousand Brahmans were assembled at that feast. Had it rested here, we should have thrived; but in the affair of the sixty, women were again murdered; in the affair of the forty, several women were murdered; the Musulmans were too strong for the Hindoos: and from that time we may trace our decline.

Q.—But you ·are a Musulman?

Lalmun.—True: but our family had been settled for two generations with that of Rae Sing and Purusram at Murnae; and had adopted their notions on all points of Thuggee. We had been first initiated by them, our family not being of the clans. Busuntee ·must have been present at the Kalee Bebee's murder.

Busuntee.—No; but my brother Punna was.

Punna—Being sent for, states—I ·was present. She was coming from Hyderabad, and was carried in a dooly, and had twelve followers. She had four thousand rupees worth of property. The Musulmans insisted upon killing her; the Hindoos opposed. She was killed with all her followers, and the Hindoos, after a desperate quarrel, consented to share in all but her clothes and ornaments. Madaree, who died last year in the Saugor jail, was the man who strangled her. On going home Purusram, Ghasee, and Himmut were obliged to give a feast, and deprecate the wrath of *Davey* by a great deal of Poojah. Five thousand Brahmans assembled at that feast, and all was well; but the Sutrooh followed, and after that the Chaleesrooh.,

In both these affairs the Hindoos consented to share, but they were sadly punished. Himmut, after the Surgooja affair, got worms in his body, and died barking like a dog. Kosul died a miserable death at Nodha. One of his sons has been transported from Saugor, and the other died in the jail. His family is extinct. Look at Purusram's family; all gone! And Ghasee Subahdar's also!

Q.—Did not the Hindoos assist in strangling the women in the Sutrooh (60) and Chaleesrooh (40) affairs?

Punna.—God forbid. They sinned enough in consenting to share in the booty, but they never assisted in the murder.

Q.—How did Feringeea get his name?

Lalmun.—General Perron could not make his uncle Rae Sing pay eighteen thousand rupees arrears due on account of his farm of the customs, and sent a regiment under Blake Sahib to seize him. The village was assaulted and burnt; and in her flight Purusram's wife gave birth to Feringeea, and he got his name from that event—Feringeea, from the attack of the Feringies.

Q.—And you think that much of your misfortunes have arisen from the murder of women?

Lalnum.—We all knew that they would come upon us some day for this and other great sins. We were often admonished but we did not take warning, and we deserve our fates.

Q.—What, for committing murder?

Lalmun.—No, but for murdering women, and those classes of people whom our ancestors never murdered.

Q.—They tell me that you were the best *Belha* (chooser of the place for murder) in your day. Was it so?

Lalmun.—I was thought a good one in my day, but I am now very old and blind. I was a man when even Khandee and Nunden were children!

Dorgha.—I got a bay pony from the Kalee Bebee's affair. My brother Punga, who died lately in the Saugor jail, and my father Khyroo, were there.

Q.—Are you never afraid of the spirits of the persons you murder?

Nasir.—Never; they cannot trouble us.

Q.—Why? Do they not trouble other men when they commit murder?

Nasir.—Of course they do. The man who commits a murder is always haunted by spirits. He has sometimes fifty at a time upon him, and they drive him mad.

Q.—And how do they not trouble you?

Nasir.—Are not the people we kill killed by the orders of *Davey?*

Kuleean.—Yes, it is by the blessing of *Davey* that we escape that evil.

Dorgha.—Do not all whom we kill go to Paradise, and why should their spirits stay to trouble us?

Inaent.—A good deal of our security from spirits is to be attributed to the roomal with which we strangle.

Q.—I did not know that there was any virtue in the roomal.

Inaent.—Is it not our sikka, (ensign) as the pick-axe is our nishan? (standard).

Feringeea.—More is attributable to the pickaxe. Do we not worship it every seventh day? Is it not our standard? Is its sound ever heard when digging the grave by any but a Thug? And can any man even swear to a falsehood upon it?

Q.—And no other instrument would answer, you think, for making the graves?

Nasir.—How could we dig graves with any other instruments. This is the one appointed by *Davey,* and consecrated, and we should never have survived the attempt to use any other.

Feringeea.—No man but a Thug who has been a strangler, and is remarkable for his cleanliness and decorum is permitted to carry it.

Q.—And there is do instance of a Thug being troubled by a spirit?

All.—None. No Thug was ever so troubled.

Q.—What became of Khimmolee to whom Newul Sing and his daughters were so much attached?

Kuleean.—He died in the Jubulpore jail.

Q.—What became of Ghubboo Khan who strangled the Moonshee's wife?

Chutter.—He also died in the Jubulpore jail.

Q.—What become of Noor Khan and his son Sadee?

Chutter.—Noor Khan died in the Huttah jail, and his son Sadee was lately transported from Jubulpore.

Q.—Were you not once arrested with a large gang at Kotah?

Feringeea.—Yes; we had murdered four men with bundles of clothes at Kunwas, going from Ashta to Kotah; and four days after we killed the nephew of Jeswunt Raw Lar, and his four servants, whose bodies were taken up last year. Twenty-eight of the gang were arrested; but the next day they had their faces blackened, and were released. I had fled, leaving my clothes behind, and after the release of the gang they discovered in my clothes the hilt of the young chief's sword, with his name written under it, and some of the cloth. In trying to overtake us they fell in with Bhimmee and Hurnagur and their gangs, and arrested forty, who were confined for four years, and released the year that the Lucknadown gang was arrested by Mr. Molony,* (1823.)

Q.—Where did you go?

Feringeea.—Ashraf Khan, Subahdar Major of Colonel Ridge's regiment of cavalry (4th Cavalry), was at Kotah, on his way home sick, the day we were released, and we followed him up and killed him and all his party.

Q.—Had he not been wounded and become an improper person to be killed?

Feringeea.—I did not go near enough to him to see. He was sick and carried in his palankeen; and my party having been arrested and had their faces blackened, we could not take any part in the murder. We got a share of the booty however.

Q.—And why did they release Hurnagur and his party?.

Feringeea.—They thought it too expensive to feed them every day.

Q.—What is commonly the proportion of Musulmans to Hindoos?

Feringeea.—In Oude nine-tenths are Musulmans. In the Dooab four-fifths were Hindoos. South of the Nurbudda three-fourths Musulmans. In Bundelcund and Saugor one-half were Musulmans. In Rajpootana one-fourth Musulmans. In Bengal, Behar, and Orissa about half and half. This is a rough guess, since we have no rule to prescribe or ascertain them.

---

* This is a mistake of *Feringeea's*—it was the year that the gang of Beg Khan was arrested by Major Wardlow—committed by Mr. Fraser, and tried by Mr. Wilder, 1826.

Q.—Arc the usages of the River Thugs the same as yours?

Moradun.—In worship the same. They strangle in boats and throw the bodies into the river. If they see blood, they must go back and open the expedition anew. They give the *Jhirnee* by striking on the neck of the boat three times, when the man appointed to give it sees all clear.

Q.—Have the River Thugs the same Ramasee (dialect) as you?

Imam Buksh, of Rustur in Ghazeepoor.—No, totally different. They neither understand our Ramasee nor do we theirs. They call a strangler Charud, and a Bcetoo, or traveller Khan, meaning their food; as we call him our Bunij, or merchandise. When they give their *Jhirnee* they say "*pawn law,*" bring paun.

Q.—Where do the River Thugs reside chiefly?

Imam Buksh.—They formerly, as I have heard my father and other old men say, constituted the exclusive population of some villages, till a Gurdee (inroad) was made upon them, and their villages were pulled down about their ears.

Q.—What was the cause of this?

Imam Buksh.—They never kill women, and there was a party of five travellers, four men and one woman, who wanted to pass across the river with them at Rajmahul. They contrived to leave the woman behind, and this led to the discovery of the murder of the men. From that time they have been scattered over the district of Burdwan, and now they live in villages occupied by other people —four or five families of them in a village.

They go in considerable parties, and have generally several boats at the ghat at the same time. The ghats most frequented by them are those of

Kohelgaum, Rajmahul, Moremukaea, an invalid
station, and Monghyr; but they go on so far as
Cawnpore, and even Furruckabad. Their murders
are always perpetrated in the day time. Those who
do the work of the boatmen are dressed like other
boatmen; but those who are to take a part in the
operations, are dressed like travellers of great
respectability; and there are no boats on the river
kept so clean, and inviting for travellers. When
going up the river they always pretend to be men
of some consideration going on pilgrimage to some
sacred place, as Banares, Allahabad, &c. When
going down they pretend to be returning home
from such places. They send out their Sothas, or
inveiglers, well dressed upon the high roads, who
pretend to be going by water to the same places
as the travellers they fall in with. On coming to
the ghat they see these nice looking boats with the
respectably dressed Thugs amusing themselves.
They ask the Manjee (captain) of the boat to take
them and the travellers on board, as he can afford
to do so cheaper than others, having apparently
his boat already engaged by others. He pretends
to be pushed for room, and the Thugs pretend to
be unwilling to have any more passengers on board.
At last he yields to the earnest requests of their
inveiglers, and the travellers are taken up. They
go off into the middle of the river, those above
singing and playing and making a great noise,
while the travellers are murdered inside at the
signal given by three taps, that all is clear, and
their bodies are thrown into the river. The boat
then goes on to some other ghat, having landed
their inveiglers again upon the roads.

Q.—How many of these river Thugs do you
suppose there are?

Imam `Buksh.—I have never served with them ·but once, and cannot say; perhaps from two hundred to two hundred and fifty.

Q.—Have you ever served with the Motheeas ?

Imam Buksh.—I have. · They are from a class of weavers or Tantooas : their Ramasee or dialect is the same as ours; they are called Motheeas by their associate Thugs, but by other people they are known only as Tantooas. I have however seen very little of them ; others here know more than I do about them ; ask Bukhtawur.

Q.—Have you seen the Lodahas ?

Imam Buksh.—Yes ; they are descended from the same common stock as ourselves, and are Jumaldehees, and Musulmans. Their dialect and usages are all the same as ours, but they rarely make Thugs of any men but the members of their own families. They marry into other families, who do not know them to be Thugs, but their wives never know their secrets, and can therefore never divulge them. No prospect of booty could ever induce them, or any of the Bengal or Behar Thugs to kill a woman.

Q.—Where do they chiefly reside ?

Imam Buksh.—They occupy some villages northeast of Durbunga on the Nepaul frontier. They emigrated from Oude when annoyed on some occasion some generations ago ; part of the emigrants remained in the Goruckpore district, and have spread to that of Chupra. They have every where followed the same trade of Thuggee ; and, as in other parts, all under the auspices of *Davey.* It was about five generations ago that this emigration from Oude took place. The Lodahas extend their expeditions from the city of Patna along all the roads leading through Dinjapore,

14*

Rungpoore, Titaleea, Durbhunga, Poruneca, Dibeea, Nathpore, and up to the banks of the Burhampootre, but I never served with them during more than one expedition. Bukhtawur knows more about them than I do. They cannot speak the language of the western provinces, and in consequence never go west of the city of Patna.

Q.—What castes are you forbidden to kill?

Imam Buksh.—We never kill any of the following classes:

Dhobies or Washermen.

Bharts or Bards.

Siks are never killed in Bengal.

Nanuksahees.

Mudaree Fukeers.

Dancing men or boys.

Musicians by profession.

Bhungies or sweepers.

Teylies, oil venders.

Lohars and *Burheys*, blacksmiths and carpenters, when found together.

Maimed and leprous persons.

A man with a cow.

Burhumcharies.

Kawrutties, or Ganges water carriers, while they have the Ganges water actually with them. If their pots be empty, they are not exempted.

Bukhtawur being sent for:

Q.—You are said to have occasionally gone with the river Thugs; what do you call them?

Bukhtawur.—We call them *Pungoos.* On one occasion only have I ever served with them.

Q.—What was the said occasion?

Bukhtawur.—About fourteen years ago I had been on an expedition from Chupra to Moorshedabad. We were twenty-two Thugs, under Sewbuns Jemadar, who was a Rajpoot. Two of our gang, Khoda Buksh and Alee Yar, had often served with the river Thugs, and used to interest us by talking about their modes of proceeding. On the other side of Rajmahul we fell in with two of these Thugs. They had two bundles of clothes, and pretended to be going on a pilgrimage, and had with them five travellers, whom they had picked up on the road. Sewbuns recognised them immediately, and Alee Yar and Khoda Buksh found in them old acquaintances. They got into conversation with them, and it was agreed that Sewbuns, I, and Dhorda Kormee should go with them, and see how they did their work, while the rest of the gang went on along the bank of the river. We embarked at Rajmahul. The travellers sat on one side of the boat and the Thugs on the other, while we were all three placed in the stern, the Thugs on our left and the travellers on our right. Some of the Thugs dressed as boatmen were above deck, and others walking along the bank of the river, and pulling the boat by the goon, or rope ; and all at the same time on the look out. We came up with a gentleman's pinnace and two baggage boats, and were obliged to stop and let them get on. The travellers seemed anxious, and were quieted by being told that the men at the rope were tired, and must take some refreshment. They pulled out something and began to eat ; and when the pinnace had got on a good way they resumed their work, and our boat proceeded. It was now afternoon, and when a signal was given above that all was clear, the five Thugs who sat opposite the travellers, sprung in upon them and with the aid of others strangled them. They put the roomal round the neck from the front, while all other

Thugs put it round from behind; they thus push them back, while we push them forward. Having strangled the five men, they broke their spinal bones, and pounded their private parts; and then threw them out of a hole made at the side into the river; and kept on their course, the boat being all this time pulled along by the men on the bank.

The booty amounted to about two ·hundred rupees. We claimed and got a share for all our party; and Sewbuns declared that we were twenty-nine, while we were really only twenty-three, and got a share for that number; he cheated them out of the share of six men.

We landed that night and rejoined. our gang, and operated upon the roads leading along the river Ganges till we got to the Mormukaeea ghat where there is an invalid station—about four cose the other side of Bar. Here we fell in with the same party of *Pungoos,* or river Thugs, who had three travellers with them. I did not join them this time, but Sewbuns with two other members of our gang went on board, and saw them strangled. What share he got I do not know.

Q.—Where do they reside?

Bukhtawur.—They reside about Beerbhoom, Bancoora, Kulna-Kutooa, Sewree and other places in the district of Burdwan, which is a very large district. Kulna and Kutooa are two distinct towns on the Bhageeruttee river, half way from Calcutta to Moorshedabad, though we always join their names together in speaking of the place. Thugs do not live in these or any other towns, as they are there always liable to be a good deal annoyed by police questions, but in small villages around about them.

Q.—What do you call police questions?

Bukhtawur.—Questions about who's come; who's gone; who's born; who's died; what's your occupation; whence your income, and so forth. These questions annoy Thugs a good deal, and oblige them to share their incomes with the police men as well as with the Zumeendars.

Q.—What's your age?

Bukhtawur.—Between sixty and seventy.

Q.—Was your father a Thug?

Bukhtawur.—No; I am the first of my family, but Iman Buksh is an hereditary Jumaldehee Thug. I was taught the trade by Manickrae Rajpoot, a Jemadar of Thugs. Both he and his son Kishun are now dead. Manickrae had lived with several families of Thugs in the village of Seesooa in Beteea, but a native collector came and gave them a good deal of annoyance, and they went to a small village near Julloo, ten cose this side of Junuckpore. I live in Pherirdaha, from Goruck-pore sixteen cose east, from the great Gunduk river nine cose west, and from the little Gunduk one cose east.

Q.—Does not the Rajah of Beteea encourage the residence of Thugs?

Bukhtawur.—Not now; he is afraid, and tries all he can to find them out and expel them; but he has got the most expert thieves in India; they will steal the bullocks from your plough without your perceiving them.

Q.—Have you ever served with the Lodahas?

Bukhtawur.—Yes. I have often served with Jhoulee Khan Jemadar. He lives thirty cose from Durbhunga on the frontier, and has thirty good Thugs. He is ostensibly a mere cultivator. He is called Jhoulee Khan the fair. There is also the black Jhoulee Khan, who has fifteen good Thugs, and holds a village in farm as a Zumeendar, though he is not so great a man as the other. Their followers are all hereditary and well trained Thugs. Jhubbun Khan, another leader of great note, lives near them. They reside in five or six villages within a few cose of each other, and are about fifty families of Thugs, most of them Musulmans, but there are some Rajpoots and some Tantooas, or weavers. These fifty families have perhaps from two hundred to two hundred and fifty Thugs.

Q.—Are your gangs never arrested in that quarter?

Bukhtawur.—Sometimes: about ten years ago a gang of seventeen were arrested near Durbhunga; four were hung, and twelve transported.

Q.—How was that managed?

Bukhtawur.—Gobind Rawut, son of Peearee Rawut, and Gheena Khan Jemadars, and a gang of fifteen Thugs had strangled and buried four travellers. Syfoo and Gheena Khan had married two sisters, and Syfoo gave himself airs, and demanded a coral necklace that was taken from one of the travellers. Gheena refused to give it; a quarrel ensued, and Syfoo, in a passion, went to the Thanadar at Durbhanga, brought him and his guard down upon them at night, and seized the whole gang. But Syfoo had not seen the grave, and he made the Thanadar tie up his cousin, Peerbuksh, a boy, throw him down, draw his sword, and pretend to be about to cut his throat. The boy got alarmed, confessed, and pointed out the grave. The bodies were taken up, the prisoners sent to Mozufurpore, and the four men who strangled them were hung; twelve, including the two leaders, were sent to the black water. Syfoo was released, but died on his way home. How, we could never discover.

Q.—Did he die because he disclosed?

Bukhtawur.—No doubt.

Q.—That is, some of his old associates killed him?

Bukhtawur.—No; had he been killed by them we should have discovered it. In those days a man who peached was either killed by his old associates, or by *Davey.* They were only rare and solitary instances; now we do not fear, as we are many and become servants of government. Syfoo must have perished for his treachery, but he was not killed by any of us.

Q.—Where were the four men murdered?

Bukhtawur.—About half a cose east of the Kolesuree river, a sacred stream, about two cose east from Durbunga.

Q.—What year was it in?

Bukhtawur.—I don't know; about ten years ago.

Moradun of Arah.—It must have been after the siege of Bhurtpore, for I saw Gheena Khan that year on an expedition. He resided near Jugtowlee in Chupra, not far from Bukhtawur's village of Phurindha.

CONVERSATION RESUMED WITH THE DUCKUN AND HINDOS-TANEE THUGS.

Q.—If *Davey's* displeasure visits all who punish Thugs, how is it that you all escape so well?

Moradun.—Davey's anger visited us when we *were seized.* That was the effect of her resentment; she cast us off then and takes no notice of us now.

Q.—And if you were to return to Thuggee, she´ would still guide and protect you?

Moradun.—Yes, but what gang would now receive us?

Q.—And are you not afraid to assist.in suppressing Thuggee?

Moradun.—No; we see God is assisting you, and that *Davey* has withdrawn her protection on account of our transgressions. We have sadly neglected her worship. God knows in what it will all end.

Q.—True, God only knows; but we hope it will end in the entire suppression of this wicked and foolish system; and in the conviction on your part that *Davey* has really had nothing to do with it.

Nasir.—That *Davey* instituted Thuggee, and supported it as long as we attended to her omens, and observed the rules framed by the wisdom of our ancestors, nothing in the world can ever make us doubt.

Q.—Do the five divisions you mention in the Duckun comprise, geographically, all the country south of the Nurbudda river?

Sahib Khan.—No, there is a sixth, Khandiesh; but we know of no Thugs in that country; and a seventh, the Concan along the Malabar coast; we know of no Thugs in that country either.

Q.—Are there no Thugs in these two districts think you?

Sahib.—There may be some, but we do not know of any.

Feringeea.—Our gangs from Hindostan used often to go through Khandiesh in our expeditions, but we never heard of any Thugs who resided there: many may have emigrated into that quarter from others since this pursuit began.

Q.—You got some valuable prizes in Khandiesh latterly?

Chotee.—There was the Choupura case on the Taptee river, in which we got 25,000 rupees in 1826.

The Dholcea and Malagaum case in which we got twenty-two thousand rupees worth of gold in 1827. The Dhorecote case in which we got twelve thousand rupees in 1828, and the Dhoree case in 1829, in which they got seventy-two thousand rupees worth of pearls, and ten thousand rupees worth of gold, though they could not keep it all. These were our prizes in Khandiesh.

Q.—You were not in the Dhoree case?

Chotee.—No, but I was in all the others. I was in arrest with Dhun Raj Seth's Agent at Alumpore, trying to recover some of the Spanish dollars taken from him at Burwaha ghat, when that occurred; but I sent part of my gang that year with Feringeea's, and they fell in with the Dhoree case men as they were coming back with the pearls.

Feringeea.—Yes; some of Chotee's men were with me in the Ranjuna case, which took place in March, 1829; and we soon after fell in with some of our friends coming home with their pearls from the Dhoree case.

Q.—But the Dhoree case and Burwaha ghat case must have taken place within a few days of each other in February, 1829; the Dhorec case took place on the 6th, and the Burwaha ghat case, on the 1st of that month. We have the records of the dates from Indore?

Chotee.—Your records must be wrong. The Dhorecote case, in which I was present, occurred fifteen days after the Burwaha ghat case, for I was taken up on the suspicion of being present in the

Burwaha ghat case, and it was the year after that. the pearls were taken at Dhoree.

Feringeea.—Yes; Chotee was with Dhun Raj Seth's man Bearee Lal when we went on the Ranjuna expedition and met the pearls.

Moklal.—He was arrested soon after our party got the Spanish dollars at Burwaha ghat, which was fifteen days before his party took the gold at Dhorecote.

Q.—How many Spanish dollars did you get?

Moklal.—We got forty thousand rupees worth, but a great part had been beaten up.

Feringeea.—But none of us got so fine a prize as Bowanee the Sooseea and his gang of Rajpootana got in Khandiesh. They carried off clear in one affair above two lakhs of rupees worth of property coming from Bombay to Indore. .

Q.—How did you manage the Burwaha ghat affair?

Moklal.—It gave us a great deal of trouble, as the dollars were laden on camels. They went fast, and, afraid to appear near to them in a body, we several times lost all trace of them. We first fell in with them at Borhanpore. Ours was only one of three great parties that went from Bundelcund, Gwalior and Saugor that year to Khandiesh; and it consisted of about one hundred and sixty Thugs, concentrating upon the treasure party. At Bur-waha ghat, on the Nurbudda river, we found them disputing with the custom-house officers about the payment of duties; and stating the hardship of being obliged to expose the value of their charge in an unsettled country. We paid duties for ourselves and our six ponies; and, leaving a few scouts, passed over the river, and went on to the small deserted village of Naen, in the midst of a jungly waste. Here we waited till the treasure party came up, consisting of eight men, mounted on camels and armed with matchlocks, and a merchant, by name Futteh Alec, who had joined them on the road in the hope of being more secure in their company than alone. It was about nine o'clock in the morning when they reached the place. The signal was given, we rushed in upon the camels, seized them by their bridles, and made them sit down by beating them with sticks. The men were seized and killed; some strangled, some stabbed with spears, and some cut down with swords. Futteh Alec was pulled off his pony and strangled. We transferred the treasure to our ponies; threw the bodies into a ravine, and went on for three days without halting any where, as we knew we should be immediately pursued. After we had got beyond danger we rested and divided the booty, setting aside the proper share for the temple of *Davey* at Dindachul, near Mirzapore.

Dhun Raj Seth sent his agent, Bearee Lal, to the Resident at Indore, and the agent of the Governor General in Bundelcund to recover his dollars. He got a good many of the principal Thug leaders arrested; they were sent by the agent in Bundelcund to the Resident at Indore, who sent them back to the agent, who made them over to the native chiefs, in whose jurisdiction they resided, with orders to make good the money. These chiefs told us to make good three-fourths of the money taken at Burwaha ghat by a general contribution. We agreed to do so and were let go; some paid out of the fruits of former expeditions, others borrowed in anticipation of future success; and those who had neither money nor credit pledged them-

selves to pay part of their future earnings. To
this Bearee Lal agreed, and sent them on expeditions, retaining Chotee, Bukut and other Jemadars
of great influence about his person.   He got a good
deal of money by procuring the release of all the
noted Thugs then in confinement at different places.
He got nine thousand rupees for the release of
Dhurum Khan Jemadar from Gwalior, on the pretence that he was engaged in the affair when he
had been in prison long before.   He had got a
great prize of jewels from some men killed near
Kotah, and his family could afford to pay.   Such
was Dhun Raj Seth's influence that he could get a
gang released from prison in any part of India;
and for some time his agent Bearee Lal had always
half a dozen of the principal Thug leaders about
his person, and used to attend all our marriages
and festivals.   What his master got, we know not,
but he got a great deal of our money.

Q.—What became of him after our operations
began?

Moklal.—He ran off to his master at Omrowtee:
we returned to our homes and got all arrested. .

Q.—Are there any Thugs in Guzerat?

Moklal.—We think not.   We have often gone
through Guzerat in our expeditions of late years;
particularly since your operations commenced, and
have penetrated beyond Joonagur up to the shores
of the ocean, but have never become acquainted
with any Thug residing in Guzerat.   There are
numbers in Rapjootana.   The Thugs of Deogur
Mudara are to Oudeepore, what the Sindouse and
Murnae men were to Etawa and Gwalior.   In
Joudhpore there are ten villages occupied by
Thugs; and they are scattered all over Jypore,

and are still very numerous about Ojeyn and Per-
tabjur in western Malwa.

Q.—But you think that a number of the members
of your old gangs who have escaped us may go
and settle in Guzerat and Khandiesh?

Moklal.—Certainly some of them will. Is not
Rambuksh for whom you offered five hundred
rupees reward gone to that quarter?

Q.—And they will raise new gangs there you
think?

Moklal.—Certainly, if left undisturbed for a time

Q.—Who were the leaders in the Burwaha g ha
affair?

Moklal.—Roshun, who was hung at Saugor,
1832.

Dhurun Khan, the stutterer, hung at Saugor,
1832.

Maharaj Partuk, who drowned himself at Saugor, 1832.

Persaud, hung at Saugor, 1832.

Lal Mahommud, approver.

Bukhtawur, who died at home.

Bukut, the son of old Khadeea approver, who is
still at large and a Jemadar.

Q.—How did you manage the Dholeea and
Malagow affair?

Feringeea.—Our gangs concentrated at the vil-
lage of Jokur, between Dholeea and Malagow, in
Khandeish, amounting to two hundred and fifty
Thugs under myself.

Makun, who was hung at Indore, 1829.

Gunga Deen, who was hung at Indore, 1829.

Chotee, approver.

Maharaj Partuk, drowned himself at Saugor.

Sheikh Nungoo, dead.

Persaud, hung at Saugor 1832, and others,

15*

We left Jokeer for Malagow with two travellers, whom we had killed before daylight and were resting at a well two cose north of Malagow, when we heard after sunrise, the *Chimmama* on the right. I proposed, according to all the recognized rules of augury, to go back to Jokur immediately. To this proposal they would not consent, and we went on to Malagow, where I proposed that we should halt and avert the threatened evil by a sacrifice. This was overruled by a party who supposed that it might be as well averted by quitting the high road to Kopurgow, and diverging to the right upon that of Chandore. I went on with them four cose to a village, whose name I forget, but at night determined to obey the omen, and came back with my gang of twenty-five Thugs to Malagow, where I found a gang of one hundred Thugs under the following leaders :

Omrow, hung at Indore, 1829.

Bhimmee, approver.

Budoloo, hung at Saugor, 1832.

Bukut, approver.

Kunhey Aheer, killed in Joudpore, 1833.

Hinder Benguna, approver.

They had with them four treasure bearers from Poona on their way from Indore, whom they intended to kill on the way to Dholeea. I joined them and we went on to the village of Jokur, and were joined on the way by three other travellers, whom we could not shake off. Hinder Benguna's son Chiddee had quarrelled with his father, and gone off to join Chotee's party on the Chandore road with Gurhoo, who went to see two of his brothers who were with them; and they having let out the secret of the treasure bearers, Chotee came off as fast as he could with Maharaj and a party of forty, and joined us during the night at Jokur.

Omrow's party was composed chiefly of Kuboolas, fellows of all casts, whom he had scraped together to make up a gang for this expedition, and we insisted upon his sending thirty of the rawest of them in advance from Jokur in the afternoon. There were at least two hundred men that night at Jokur on their way back from Hindostan to their regiments; but we watched the treasure bearers closely, and when they set out, we followed; and at a bowlee, a mile or two on, we closed in upon them and put them to death. We had not been able to shake off the other three travellers, and were in consequence obliged to put them to death also, some of the bodies were thrown into the bowlee, and the others were slightly buried in a field close by.

Chotee claimed a share for that part of their gangs which had gone on to Chandore, as well as for that which had come with him; and Omrow claimed an equal share for all the thirty Kuboolas whom he had consented to send on in advance, that they might not by their blunders frustrate our designs upon the treasure bearers. After a good deal of dispute it was settled that those who were actually present, should all share alike without distinction of rank or office; and that those who belonged to absent parties might share what they got with them or not as they pleased. According to this arrangement each man got of gold one hundred and twenty-five rupees worth. Omrow's seventy men afterwards shared with the thirty Kuboolas: and Chotee's party went and shared what they got with the men at Chandore.

Q.—And you think the *Chimmama* was sent to

you by *Davey* to induce you all to stay and share in this booty?

Feringeea. — Undoubtedly; every one now admits it, but at the time they were all mad!

Q. — Why did they not diverge immedietely from the Malagow road?

Feringeea. — It is all a horrid Jungle, and there is no road right or left till you get to Malagow. We had intended to go the straight road to the Kopurgow through Malagow.

Q. — Who were the three travellers that joined you?

Feringeea. — Two were weavers, and one a dawk hurcara.

Q. — How was the Dhoree affair managed.

Feringeea. — We were a gang of about one hundred and fifty Thugs from Hindostan; in the month of January, 1829, near Chopra, on the bank of the Taptee river, under Khoseeala, alias Rymoo, executed afterwards at Dholeea in Khandiesh. Bhujjoo, executed at Saugor, 1832, and Persaud Musulman, executed at Indore, 1829, when the seven treasure bearers came up on their way from Bombay to Indore. We followed them with a select party from all the gangs on the Dhoree, and thence through the Dholeebaree pass, where they spoke with Dusrut Naek, the officer of the police guard, stationed at that pass. While they rested here, one of the seven, without our scouts perceiving it, went on in advance towards Godurghat, which is about four cose distant. When they had left the guard we continued to follow, and on passing the guard we were questioned, by Dusrut Neak, and we told him that we were government servants on our way home on furlough. About half way between this pass and Godurghat we came up with the treasure bearers, and strangled

them ; but to our surprise we found only six instead
of seven. Heera and three others were instantly
sent on after the other but they could not find him,
and we hastily threw the bodies into a nalah and
made off with the booty.

The man who had gone on in advance, finding
that his companions did not come up so soon as
he expected, returned to look after them, and met
a traveller, who told him that he had seen some
dead bodies in a nalah by the side of the road ;
going to the place described he found that they
were the bodies of his companions, and reported
the circumstance to Dusrut Neak, who sent information to Captain Hodges, the acting magistrate
in Khandeish, and set out with all his men in pursuit
of us. Captain Hodges with his mounted police,
succeeded in seizing thirteen or fourteen of our
party who had separated and lost their road in
the jungles. They had with them the greater part
of the booty, which we in consequence lost. Of
these men four contrived to get released, and the
rest were either hung at Dholeea or sent to the
black water. Only three of the bags of pearls
were brought off, one by Purumna, who honestly
shared it on his return with the rest of the gang
who escaped ; and two by Bhujjoo, alias Sooper
Sing and Rae Sing, who were lately hung at Saugor, and who could never be prevailed upon to
give up any share.

Q.—When you have a poor traveller with you,
or a party of travellers who appear to have little
property about them, and you hear or see a very
good omen, do you not let them go, in the hope
that the virtue of the omen will guide you to better
prey ?

Dorgha, Musulman. — Let them go ! never,
never ; *kubhee nuheen, kubhee nuheen.*

Nasir, Musulman, of Telingana.—How could we let them go? Is not the good omen the order from Heaven to kill them, and would it not be disobedience to let them go? If we did not kill them, should we ever get any more travellers?

Feringeea, Brahmun.—I have known the experiment tried with good effect. I have known travellers who promised little let go, and the virtue of the omen brought better.

Inaent, Musulman.—Yes, the virtue of the omen remains, and the traveller who has little should be let go, for you are sure to get a better.

Sahib Khan, of Telingana.—Never! never! This is one of your Hindostanee heresies. You could never let him go without losing all the fruits of your expedition. You might get property, but it could never do you any good. No success could result from your disobedience.

Morlee, Rajpoot.—Certainly not! the travellers who are in our hands when we have a good omen must never be let go, whether they promise little or much; the omen is unquestionably the order, as Nasir says.

Nasir.—The idea of securing the good will of *Davey* by disobeying her order is quite monstrous. We Duckun Thugs do not understand how you got hold of it. Our ancestors were never guilty of such folly.

Feringeea.—You do not mean to say that we of Murnae and Sindouse were not as well instructed as you of Telingana?

Nasir and *Sahib Khan.*—We only mean to say that you have clearly mistaken the nature of a good omen in this case. It is the order of *Davey* to take what she has put in our way: at least so we, in the Duckun, understand it.

Q.—How did you manage the Shikarpore affair?

Inaent.—Our gang consisted of one hundred and twenty-five Thugs under,

Noor Khan, hung this year at Jubulpore.

Bhudae, lately arrested at Kotah.

Gholab Khan, hung at Saugor 1832.

Hyput, aprover.

Other Jemadars and myself were encamped in the grove near the town of Sehora in this, the Jubulpore district, in March, 1816, when the Resident of Nagpore passed on his way from Nagpore to Bundelcund.* We had heard of his approach with a large escort and determined to join his party in the hope of picking up some travellers, as in the time of the Pindaries, travellers of respectability generally took advantage of such opportunities to travel with greater security. Our gang separated into small parties, who mixed themselves up with the Resident's parties at different places along the road, without appearing to know any thing of each other ; and pretended to be like others glad of the occasion to travel securely. When the Resident reached Belehree some of our parties stated, that, as the Resident was going the western road by Rewah, they had better go the northern by Powae, as there was no longer any danger from Pindaries, and, by separating from so large an escort, they should get provisions much cheaper; that water was now becoming scarce on the western road, and was always made dirty by the elephants and camels. Other parties pretended to argue against this, but at last to yield to the strong reasons assigned. We had by this time become very

* This was Major Close, on his way from Poona to Gwalior, to take charge of his office as Resident, in 1816.

intimate with a party of travellers from Nagpore, consisting of eighteen men, seven women, and two boys. They heard our discussions, and declared in favour of the plan of separating from the Resident's party, and going the northern road through Shikarpore and Powae.

On reaching Shikarpore, three cose this side of Powae, we sent on Kunhey and Mutholee to select a place for the murder, and they chose one on the bank of the river in an extensive jungle that lay between us and Powae. We contrived to make the party move off about midnight persuading them that it was near morning; and on reaching the place appointed they were advised to sit down and rest themselves. All our parties pretended to be as much deceived as themselves with regard to the time; but not more than half of the travellers could be prevailed upon to sit down and rest in such a solitude. The signal was given, and all, except the two boys, were seized and strangled by the people who had been appointed for the purpose, and were now at their posts ready for action. The boys were taken by Jowahir and Kehree, who intended to adopt them as their sons; and the bodies of the twenty-five persons were all thrown into a ditch, and covered over with earth and bushes. On seeing the bodies thrown into the ditch, Jowahir's boy began to cry bitterly; and finding it impossible to pacify him or to keep him quiet, Jowahir took him by the legs, dashed out his brains against a stone, and left him lying on the ground, while the rest were busily occupied in collecting the booty. Going on to Powae we purchased five rupees worth of sugar to celebrate this event; and without halting we went on to the village of Choumooka in Punna. After resting till

midnight we went on to Tigura, in Jytpore, where
where we ate the sugar, and then set out the same
day for Huttah. ·

A fisherman going to the river to fish, soon after
we had left the scene of the murders, found the
body of the boy lying by the stone against which
his head had been beaten; and he gave information to
Thakur Burjore Sing of Powae, who proceeded to
the place with some of his followers, and discovered all the other bodies lying in the ditch. He
collected all the men he could, and following our
traces which were still fresh, he came up with us
as we were washing ourselves in a stream within
the boundaries of the village of Tigura. We formed
ourselves into a compact body, and retired upon
the village of Tigura. The Thakur repeatedly
charged in upon us, and seeing Hyput Jamadar
pierced through the chest with a spear, and Bhugwan receive a sabre cut in the face, we dispersed
and made for the village of Tigura in the best way
we could. The villagers all came to our support,
and defended us against the Thakur; but he had
already secured Husun Khan, who afterwards died
at home, Imam Buksh, alias Kosula, who was
hung in Khandiesh in 1829, Shumshera, who was
hung at Saugor in 1832, and Bahadera, who is
now in service at Hingolee.

The Tigura people tempted by the promise of
part of our booty, protected us all that day and
night; and in the morning escorted us to Simareea,
where a promise of all the booty that we had left,
secured us a safe retreat till the pursuit was over,
in spite of all that the Thakur could say or do.

The Thakur took all his prisoners to the governor general's agent, Mr. Wauchope, before whom
Bahadera confessed, and stated all the circumstan-

ces as they occurred; but being afterwards told that it was the practice of the English to hang all who confessed, and to release all who denied,- he soon denied stoutly all that he had said, and pretended to know nothing at all about the murders; and being made over to the magistrate, they were all released for want of evidence. Ram Buksh Tumbolee came from Nagpore to the Agent, Mr. Wauchope, in the hope of recovering his child, who was the boy that was killed by Jowahir.*

Q.—What became of Jowahir?

Inaent.—He was the Jowahir Kusbatee the Brāhmun, who was hung at Saugor, 1832. He had settled on the Norbudda river.

Q.—What became of Kehree?

Inaent.—Kehree was the father of Sewa, approver, and he was hung at Jubulpore in 1831. He named the boy Gunesha, and kept him at home to look after his cattle. Kehree's widow is now here with her son Sewa; and I heard her some time ago lamenting the death of Gunesha, and performing funeral ceremonies. The boy was a Brahmun and died at Kehree's home.

Q.—Where is Bahadera?

Inaent.—The last time I saw him was about ten years ago, when he was a Sipahee in the 1st battalion of a brigade of five battalions at Aurungabad. He had given up Thuggee, and never, that we know of, returned to it; but he was still our friend.

Q.—You told Mr. Johnstone the traveller, while he was at Saugor, that the operations of your trade were to be seen in the caves of Ellora?

Feringeea.—All! Every one of the operations is to be seen there: in one place you see men

---

* This is all strictly true.

strangling : in another burying the bodies ; in another carrying them off to the graves. There is not an operation in Thuggee that is not exhibited in the caves of Ellora.

Dorgha.—In those caves are to be seen the operations of every trade in the world.

Chotee.—Whenever we passed near, we used to go and see these caves. Every man will there find his trade described, however secret he may think it ; and they were all made in one night.

Q.—Does any person beside yourselves consider that any of those figures represent Thugs ?

Feringeea.—No body else ; but all Thugs know that they do. We never told any body else what we thought about them. Every body there can see the secret operations of his trade, but he does not tell others of them ; and no other person can understand what they mean. They are the works of God. No human hands were employed upon them. That every body admits.

Q.—What particular operations are there described in figures ?

Sahib Khan.—I have seen the Sotha (inveigler) sitting upon the same carpet with the traveller, and in close conversation with him, just as we are when we are worming out their secrets. In another place the strangler has got his roomal over his neck, and is strangling him ; while another, the Chumochee, is holding him by the legs. These are the only two operations that I have seen described.

Nasir.—These I have also seen, and there is no mistaking them. The Chumochee has close hold of the legs, and is pulling at them *thus,* while the Bhurtote is tightening the roomal round his neck, *thus !*

Q.—Have you seen no others ?

Feringeea.—I have seen these two, and also the Lughas carrying away the bodies to the grave, *in this manner*, and the sextons digging the grave with the sacred pick-axe : all is done just as if we had ourselves done it; nothing could be more exact.

Q.—And who do you think could have, executed this work ?

Feringeea.—It could not have been done by Thugs, because they would never have exposed the secrets of their trade; and no other human being could have done it. It must be the work of the Gods : human hands could never have performed it.

Q.—And supposing so, you go and worship it ?

Sahib Khan.—No. We go to gratify curiosity, and not to worship ; we look upon it as a Mausoleum, a collection of curious figures cut by some demons, who knew the secrets of all mankind, and amused themselves here in describing them.

Hurnagur.—We Hindoos go for the same purpose. We never go to worship. We consider it as a Pantheon of unknown Gods.

Q.—Relate the circumstances of the Chaleesrooh affair ?

Kuleean Sing.—In the year that Mr. Jenkins went as Resident to Nagpore through Benares and Sumbulpore, this affair took place. He had just encamped near the Seetabuldee hill when we passed through Nagpore. (February, 1807.)

Dorgka.—The roads from the Duckun across the Nurbudda, had become so unsafe from the Pindaries that all travellers from Poona, Hyderabad, and Nagpore, going towards the Ganges, went by way of Surgooja and Sumbulpore ; and several of

our gangs that went from Bundelcund and the
Dooab to that road came back with immense booty
for several years. In the rains preceding this affair
it was determined that all the gangs should take
that direction; and we accordingly set out. There
were more than forty Jemadars of note; among
them Bukshee Jemadar, whose head Doctor Spry
sent to England, and Ghasee Subahdar; and many
others of equal note. We set out from our respective homes after the Dushera in October, (1806)
passed through Mirzapore, in order to make our
votive offerings at the temple of *Davey* at Binda-
chul, and rendezvoused at Ruttunpore in the Surgooja district, where we were assembled above six
hundred Thugs. From Ruttunpore we went to
Tukutpore, where we murdered a good many
travellers who took up their quarters in our several
places of encampment. All pretended to have been
on furlough and to be returning from Hindostan to
different armies in the Duckun, with some of our
relations and friends as young recruits. On the
third day a female of rank came up. Her husband
had been an officer in the Nagpore service, and
being left a widow by his death at Nagpore, she
was on her way home to her friends with her
deceased husband's brother. She occupied a tent,
and was accompanied by a slave girl, and had
twelve armed men as a guard. She left Tukutpore the morning after her arrival, and was followed
by a detachment from every one of our gangs,
making a party of one hundred and sixty Thugs,
under some of our best leaders. For several days
they followed them without finding a convenient
opportunity of disposing of them, till they reached
the village of Choora, between which place and

16*

the village of Sutrunja the road passed through an extensive jungle, without a village on either side for many miles. Leaving this place in the morning they put the whole party to death, and buried their bodies in a nalah. I did not go with this party.

When they set out after the widow, we all proceeded towards Nagpore; and on reaching Lahnjee, a party of sixty Thugs remained there, while the rest went on towards Nagpore. I'remained with the sixty at Lahnjee, and two days after the main body had left us, a party of forty travellers came up on their way to the Ganges; thirty-one men, seven women, and two girls. The greater part of these people were from Ellichpore; the rest from Nagpore. Our Jemadars soon became intimate with the principal men of this party, pretended to be going to the same parts of India, and won their confidence; and the next day we set out with them, and in four days reached Ruttunpore, where we met the party of one hundred and sixty Thugs returning after the murder of the widow and her party. They did not, however, appear to be known to us. Soon after, two hundred of the main body, who had gone on towards Nagpore from Lahnjee, came up, having heard of the forty travellers soon after they left us; and all pretended to be going the same road, without appearing to have any acquaintance with each other. It was, however, agreed that sixty, of the one hundred and sixty, should go on and rejoin the party who had proceeded to Nagpore, leaving three hundred and sixty to dispose of this party.

From Ruttunpore, we proceeded with the party of travellers to the village of Choora, whence we sent on people to select a proper place for the murder. They chose one not far from that in which the widow and her party had been put to death. Durroo and Sheera were sent on to the village of Sutrunja to see that all was clear in front; and about a watch and half before daylight we set out with the travellers, leaving scouts behind to see that we were not interrupted from the rear. By the time we reached the appointed place the Bhurtotes and Shumseeas had all on some pretext or other got close by the side of the persons whom they were appointed to strangle; and on reaching the spot the signal was given in several places at the same time, and thirty-eight out of forty were seized and strangled. The daughter of Gunga Tewaree was a very handsome young woman, and Punchum, one of our Jemadars, wished to preserve her as a wife for his son Bukholee. But when she saw her mother and father strangled, she screamed, and beat her head against the stony ground, and tried to kill herself. Punchum tried in vain to quiet her, and promised to take great care of her, and marry her to his own son who would be a great chief; but all was in vain. She continued to scream, and at last Punchum put the roomal round her neck and strangled her. The widow of Alfie's brother was strangled, but her daughter, a girl about three years of age, was preserved by Kosul Jemadar, who married her to his own son Hunnee Rae Brahmum, by whom she had two sons, one of whom is still living, and about ten or eleven years of age. Since the death of Kosul and Hunnee Rae she has lived with her husband's mother.

We buried all the bodies in a nalah, and got property to the value of about seventeen thousand rupees, which we took on with us and divided at

Sutrunja. After this affair we returned home
through Rewah and Chitterkote, the place where
we had murdered the sixty persons at one time
about two years before. The widow of Hunnee
Rae often heard, after she grew up, of the Chaleesrooh affair in which her mother and uncle were
strangled; and she has herself told you all she
knows about it.

Q.—What became of Punchum?

Dorgha.—Punchum died before we reached
home.

Q.—Had Punchum any sons?

Inaent.—Punchum had Chunderbhan, who died
on a Thug expedition; Bhugholee, hung at Gwalior
by Jacob Sahib; Jowahir who died in Gwalior;
Odeebhan hung in Khandiesh, 1829—and Mollo
who died in the Nursingpore jail.

Q.—And Kosul, what became of him?

Dorgha.—Kosul Subahdar died at his home: he
had two sons—Ajeeta who was transported from
Saugor, 1832, and Rawut Rae who died last year
in the Saugor jail. Hunnee Rae was the son of
his brother, but he had adopted him.

Q.—How long had you given up Thuggee before
you were seized?

Dorgha.—Soon after the Moghalanee affair 1821.
Saugor and all the countries along the Nurbudda
through which we used to pass in going to the
Duckun were taken by the Company, and as we
were constantly liable to be detained and asked a
number of questions, I thought I had better give up
Thuggee, otherwise I and my children might some
day get hung or sent to the black water. I accordingly entered the service of Bebee Knox, who
resides in the Orderly Bazar at Cawnpore, and has

some thirty-two villages purchased at auction, and thirteen bungalows at that station. I became one of her confidential servants, and was employed in bring her rents from her native collectors of the villages. Colonel Knox died, I believe at Futtehgur, about the year that Saugor was taken, but I never saw him. I had served her for nearly twelve years when you sent for me, and she and all the people had become attached to me, and you know what difficulty you had to get me away.

Q.—And during this time you never went on Thuggee?

Dorgha.—Never.

Q.—But your brother Kohman went, though he was in the same service.

Dorgha.—True he went, but it was very seldom that he could be persuaded to join the gangs. He went only after long intervals, and was never long absent at a time.

Q.—I thought Hindoos never strangled women. How came Punchum to strangle this girl?

Feringeea.—Punchum was my mother's brother, and he never strangled her!

Q.—Who did?

Feringeea.—I have heard that it was Bhugwan Kachee, a slave or disciple of his.

Punna.—But is not the act of the slave the act of the master? and did not Bhugwan strangle her by Punchum's order?

Feringeea.—Well, but how was Punchum punished! did he not die before he could reach home; and was not his son Bughola hung the November following, with twenty others, whom Jacob Sahib strung up at Kalapaharee in Gwalior? and was not Bhugwan hung with him—and what a horrid death did Himmut die? He was eaten alive by the worms!

Dorgha.—I myself saw Punchum strangle the young woman. Bhugwan may have assisted.

Q.—How did Jacob Sahib seize and convict this gang?

Dhorgha.—After the Surgooja affair in the month of October, a body of thirty or forty Thugs from Murnae and Sindouse, on passing near Kala-paharee, murdered three men; and soon after one of the party flogged a boy whom he had picked up some where and adopted: the boy went off to Jacob Sahib, told of the murder, and pointed out the bodies; and he seized them, and hung up twenty-one at four different places along the road.

Ameer Alee.—I was with that party. It was some years after the Surgooja expedition. I forget the name of the boy, but he belonged to Bukshee Jemadar, whose head is gone to Europe. I was employed to go forward and back with messages from the arrested Thugs to their families and friends. · Large sums were offered to Jacob Sahib for their ransom, but he would not let them go: one day I found some of them hanging upon trees, and got too much frightened to return.

Q.—You were in the Chitterkote, or as you call it, the Surtrooh (sixty soul) affair. Pray tell me what you recollect of it?

Dorgha.—After the capture of Gawilgur by General Wellesley (Duke of Wellington*) it was restored to the Nagpore Rajah, who appointed Ghureeb Sing to the command of the fortress. Anxious to get some good soldiers from Hindostan

---

* Gawilgur was taken December, 1803. This affair must have taken place 1805.

to garrison it, he sent his younger brother Ghyan Sing, with a number of followers, and a large sum of money, to raise them in the Oude country and districts between the Ganges and Jumna rivers.

Ghyan Sing and his party passed through Nagpore, and came to Jubulpore in the month of June, while we were there concentrated from the different parts into which we had extended our expeditions that season. His party consisted of fifty-two men, seven women, and a Brahmun boy, then about four years of age. Some of our gangs lodged in the town, some in the cantonments, among the troops, and some were encamped at the tank of Adhar, two or three miles from the town on the road to Mirzapore. As soon as we heard of the arrival of this party from the Duckun, every party of Thugs deputed some of its most respectable members to mix with them in the town, and win their confidence. At first they tried to separate them into different parties to proceed by different roads, but though they had collected together at different times and places on the road, it was found impossible to separate any part of them from Ghyan Sing; and we agreed to unite all our gangs, and to lead the party by the most unfrequented roads till we might find a place convenient for the murder of the whole at once.

On reaching Sehora we persuaded them to quit the high road through Belehree and Myhere, and take that through Chundeea and the old fort of Bundoogur, which leads through very extensive tracts of jungle, and uninhabited country. We went with them through all this country however without finding what we considered a fitting time and place, and reached Rewah winning more and more upon their confidence every day. From

Rewah we went to Simareea, and from that place to a small village half way to Chitterkoke, called by us the Burwala Gow, from a large Bur tree that stood near it. Thence we sent on people as usual to select a place for the murder, and they found one about two cose and a half distant, in a very extensive jungle, without a human habitation for many miles on either side. We persuaded the party to set out soon after midnight; and as they went along we managed to take our appointed places, two Thugs by every traveller, and the rest, in parties of reserve at different intervals along the line, every two managing to keep the person they were appointed to kill, in conversation. On reaching the place chosen, the signal was given at several different places, beginning with the rear party and passing on to that in front; and all were seized and strangled except the boy. It was now near morning, and too late to admit of the bodies being securely buried; we made a temporary grave for them in the bed of the river, covered them over with sand, and went on with the boy and the booty to Chitterkoke, intending to send back a large party the next night, and have the bodies securely buried. The rains had begun to set in, and after the murders it rained very heavily all the day. The party however went back, but found that the river had risen and washed away all the bodies except two or three, which they found exposed, and pushed into the stream to follow the rest.*

Q.—What became of the boy?

Dorgha.—He was brought up by Mungul Brahmun, the brother of Laljoo, and having taken to

---

* This is a very correct statement of the case.

the trade of Thuggee, he was last year sent to the black water from Saugor.

Q.—What became of Mungul and Laljoo?

Dorgha.—They both died in a village in Bhopaul where they had settled.

Q.—Chotee—You were with the party arrested by Major Henley in March, 1832, I believe?

Chotee.—Yes: we had killed five Sipahees a little on this side of Ashta, and having put them into a temporary grave, we went on, leaving nine men to bury them securely the next night. They were seized, and a party was sent after us. We were all taken, a party of sixty-three, and brought to Sehore where we were detained some days, and then sent to Mr. Maddock at Saugor. He sent us to Mr. Robinson at Cawnpore, where we were all released immediately.

Q.—Were the bodies discovered?

Chotee.—I believe so, but it was not for that affair that we were arrested. Bechoo and his party had killed three months before a Jemadar of Hurcaras, whom the Nowab of Bhopaul had sent to escort his gang from the city of Bhopaul to Major Henley's camp. They strangled him on the road, and made off. We could tell Major Henley nothing about this affair, and he sent us out of the country.

Q.—Thakur Persaud was with that gang believe?

Thakur Persaud.—Yes, I was in that gang with Bechoo. We were a party of about forty Thugs, and in the city of Bhopaul we were taken up by the Nowab's people on suspicion and sent to Major Henley the Agent, who lived three stages off at Sehore. He was at the time out on his circuit. One Jemadar of Hurcaras was sent with us, and

at a place about a cose and a half from the village
of Kuttora he was strangled by Hindoo Aheer
Jemadar, who was hung at Indore 1829, and his
body was thrown into a nalah where it lay concealed in the long grass. We went on to Sohud,
about eighteen cose from Ojeyn, where we murdered four people, and got a booty that gave to
each man a quarter of a seer of gold: it was
fifteen years ago.

Q.—Were you not of the party arrested by
Captain Waugh at Kotah in the beginning of 1822?

Hurnagur.—Yes, we had killed two Suraffs at
Patun, and were forty-four of us arrested in the
beginning of that year, a day or two after Feringea's gang had been released with their faces
smutted over. Our affair of the Suraffs had not
been discovered, and we were arrested on the sup-
position that we were part of his gang who had
been concerned in the murder of the cloth merchants at Kunwas. We were made to work on
the roads about Major Caulfield's house at Kotah
for four years and half, when he ordered us to be
released. There were two Koelcea Thugs confined with us at the same time—Imma Khan and
Soobratee.

Q.—What has become of all these forty-four
men?

Hurnagur.—There are only seven surviving
and still at large. Some have died, some been
hung, some sent to the black water, and some are
here in prison. Bhimmee Jemadar has told Mr.
McLeod all about them. He has put all their
names in a book.

10th JULY, 1835.—PRESENT, FERINGEEA BRAHMUN—AND MUDAR BUKSH, DORGHA, KAEM KHAN, MUSULMANS.

Q.—Where did you fall in with the Moghulanee?

Feringeea.—My gang consisted of about fifty persons, and returning from Joudpore to Chourcoo we fell in with the Moghulanee. It was the year before Ashraf Khan Subahdar Major and his party were murdered.* We came on to Madhoorajpore, where we fell in with the brother of a *Kuptan* in the Kuroulee Rajah's service, bringing from the Pokkar fair a fine young horse for the Rajah. We set out before daylight with him and his party, put them to death and buried their bodies about a cose distant, and came on nine cose to Charsoo.

Q—And what became of the young woman?

Feringeea.—We left her behind as we had no designs upon her; but she followed, and lodged in the Surae while we encamped on the bank of the Tank. The next day we came to Duolutpore, where we lodged with some of our Sooseea Thug friends, and the Moghulanee still followed, and lodged in the Bazar. Six of our Sooseea friends joined us here, and came on with us to Lalsont. I had tried to shake off the Moghulanee, but soon after our arrival she came up.

Q.—Where did you fall in with the Musulman party?

Feringeea.—At Lolsont. Baz Khan, Zalim, Bhimmee, Dorgha and their gangs, amounting to one hundred and twenty-five Thugs, came up from Ameergur.

Q.—What had you been doing at Ameergur?

* Ashraf Khan was murdered 1822, February.

Dorgha.—We were a large gang on our way from Ajmere to Neemuch, and having killed a good many people on the way, we reached Ameergur with a Musulman traveller, who had joined us during the last stage. Two shop-keepers came up from the Mow cantonments and lodged in our camp, and about nine o'clock at night they were all three strangled, and their bodies were wrapped up like bundles of cloth and taken by five *Lughas* to the Jheel, to the south west corner of the Fort. We were encamped on the west side. It was a moonlight night in March, and some people on the bastion saw them, and came down to see what they were about. Two out of the five men ran into our camp, and three fled in the opposite direction. The four men from the Fort, without examining the bundles, followed the two men into our camp, and demanded the thieves. They were four Meena police men, and they declared that they had seen five men making off with bundles of clothes, and as they ran into our camp, they insisted upon our giving them up. I addressed those about me in Rumasee and proposed to strangle the whole four. Punna, approver, and Molloo, lately transported, seconded me, and our roomals were ready, when the Jemadars said that it could be of no use, as others must have seen the *Lughas* at the same time, and we should have them down upon us before we could dispose of the bodies. I then told the Meenas that I could not believe them unless they showed me the bundles. They offered to do so, and we proceeded on half way to the spot, which gave the gangs time to get ready to be off, when I pretended that I was afraid to go with them alone, and would go back for my sword, and a friend or two. They went on to the bundles, and I returned to our camp.

We all made off by different roads having agreed to re-unite at Chouroo, and travelled all night and all the next day; as we met a regiment of cavalry soon after leaving camp, on their way from Ajmere to either Neemuch or Mow. We were all re-united at Chouroo five or six days after, and there we rested and divided the booty. Molloo pretended that he had thrown away in his flight all the valuables that he got from the two shop-keepers; but we suspected him. The booty acquired from eight men murdered by our different parties in their flight, was here divided with what we got from the Musulman at Ameergur.

Q.—But where did you fall in with Feringeea and the Moghulanee?

Dorgha.—We fell in with them at Lalsont and came on with them to Somp.

Q.—Who were with her?

Dorgha.—She had an old female servant, mounted upon a pony, one armed man servant, and six bearers for her palankeen. From Somp we sent on men to select a place for the murder, and set out with her before daylight; but the Belha, in the dark, lost the road, and we were trying to find it when the young woman beuame alarmed, and began to reproach us for taking her into the jungle in the dark. We told Feringeea to come up and quiet her, but dreading that some of her party might make off, the signal was given, and they were all strangled.

Q.—What did you get from them?

Dorgha.—Six hundred rupees worth of property.

Q.—And was this enough to tempt so large a gang to murder a beautiful young woman?

Dorgha.—We were very averse to it, and often

17*

said that we should not get two rupees a piece, and that she ought to be let go; but Feringeea insisted upon our *taking* her.

Q.—How did you advise the murder of a young woman like this?

Feringeea.—It was her fate to die by our hands. I had several times tried to shake them off before we met the Musulmans, and when we came to Lalsont I told her that she must go on, as I had joined some old friends, and should be delayed. She then told me that I must go to her home with her near Agra, or she would get me into trouble; and being a Brahmun while she was a Musulman, I was afraid that I should be accused of improper intercourse, and turned out of cast.

Q.—But you might have gone another road?

Dorgha.—He could not, as he had before told her that he was going to her village of Ateer near Agra; and had he left her, she might have suspected us, and got us all seized as bad characters. Khoda Buksh was placed by her as Sotha, and she told him that the young Subahdar, meaning Feringeea, should go to her home with her.

Q.—Why did she call him Subahdar?

Dorgha.—We all called him Subahdar at that time, because his cousin, Aman, was one of our Subahdars; and because he was a handsome young man, and looked like a man of rank, which was useful to us.

Q.—Had any thing improper taken place between him and the young woman?

Dorgha.—Certainly not, or we could never have killed her; but he had a good deal of conversation with her, and she had taken a great fancy to him. She was very fair and beautiful, and we should never have killed her had he not urged us to do so.

Khoda Buksh who died lately in the Saugor jail, and whose brother Rostum is with Mr. Wilson, told us that we must either kill her or let Feringeea go on with her. He would not consent to this, and we agreed to kill her.

Q.—Who strangled her?

Dorgha.—Madar Buksh, while Khoda Buksh held her down, and Feringeea assisted in pulling her from her palankeen.

Feringeea.—Dorgha knows this to be false and that I was not in sight at the time.

Dorghu.—I know we called you to pacify her when she got alarmed, and I think I saw you assisting.

Q.—Did you strangle the young woman?

Madar Buksh.—I did.

Q.—Did Feringeea assist?

Madar Buksh.—No.

Q.—You were then a young man, and she was a beautiful young woman: had you no pity?

Madar Buksh.—I had, but I had undertaken the duty, and we must all have food. I have never known any other means of gaining it.

Feringeea.—We all feel pity sometimes, but the goor of the Tuponee changes our nature. It would change the nature of a horse. Let any man once taste of that goor, and he will be a Thug though he know all the trades and have all the wealth in the world. I never wanted food; my mother's family was opulent, her relations high in office. I have been high in office myself, and became so great a favourite wherever I went that I was sure of promotion: yet I was always miserable while absent from my gang, and obliged to return to Thuggee. My father made me taste of that fatal goor when I was yet a mere boy; and if I were to live a thousand years I should never be able to follow any other trade.

Q.—Did you hear any thing about the bodies and the men from the fort of Ameergur?

Dorgha.—We heard afterwards from travellers that they were taken to Neemuch, and charged themselves with the murder and punished.

Q.—And you went after this into service at Cawnpore?

Dorgha.—Yes; I took lands at rent in the village of the Bebee and entered her service?

Q.—Who was this Moghulanee whom you killed?

Feringeea.—She had belonged to the family of Akoo Meean, the brother of Nowab Ameer Khan, but having eloped she went to the Neemuch cantonments, whence she was now on her way to the village of Ateer near Agra. .

Q.—You Kaem Khan, were with Rostum and Khoda Buksh in the Dhosa affair. Relate what you recollect of it?

Kaem Khan.—We were on our way from Madhoorajpore to Gwalior, a gang of about forty Thugs in the month of March, ten years ago, when we fell in with Bunseelal, the son of Bhujunlal, and Cotwal of Sopur. He was a lad of about seventeen years of age, and had with him two Brahmuns, one Rajpoot Sepahee and a servant of the Jat cast, and was going to Rewaree to fetch his bride. One of the Brahmuns had come from Rewaree to accompany him. They came and took up their quarters in the same Surae with us, and we pretended to be going the same road. The next morning we went on with them to Lolsont, where we again lodged together in the Surae of Kosul Bhuteeara. The following day we went on to Ramgur with them, and thence Bikka Jemadar went on to select a place for the murder, but he came back without finding one that pleased him, and the day after we went on together to Dhosa. We had now become very intimate with the boy and his party, who told us all their secrets. The boy lodged in the shop of a Buneeh who had been long in league with us, while we lodged in the Surae at Dhosa, and in the afternoon Bikka went on again to select a bele. He chose one in the bed of a nalah a cose and a half distant, and the five stranglers having been appointed, we set out with the boy and his party long before daylight the next morning. On reaching the place appointed, they were persuaded to sit down and rest themselves. The boy sat with one of the Brahmuns upon a carpet that we had spread for him, and the other three attendants sat down upon the sand at a little distance from them. A *Shumseea* took his seat by the side of each of the five, and the *Bhurtoles* stood each behind his intended victim. The signal was given by Rostum Khan, and all five were immediately strangled, the boy himself by Bhikka Jemadar, who is still at large, while his hands were held by his brother Chunda. The bodies were buried in the bed of the nalah. While they were strangling them, the fine mare on which the youth rode ran off, and while we were engaged in recovering her, Chunda made off with a purse of gold Mohurs, which he found in the boy's waist-band.

Q.—Did you not return to Doosa soon after and heard the boy's friends searching for him?

Kaem Khan.—Yes; we came back to Doosa some time after and heard from our friends the shop-keepers, that the bodies had been dug up by

Jackals, and that the friends of the murdered youth were then at Doosa inquiring about him. Going to Surae we found the uncle of the youth sitting on a Chubootra in front of the door, weeping and lamenting the loss of his nephew.

Q.—Did not the father die of grief soon after?

Kaem Khan.—Yes. He could never be persuaded to eat any thing after he learnt the fate of his only son, and soon died. This we afterwards learned from the people of Sooper who still recollect the circumstance of the loss of the son and death of old Cotwal.*

PRESENT THUKOREE, FERINGEEA, DORGHA, INAENT, LALMUN, KHARUDEE, NUNDUN.

Q.—You were, I believe, Thukoree, among the Thugs arrested after the murder of Lieut. Monsell in the end of 1812?

Thukoree Aheer.—I was, and we were kept in prison thirteen months and horribly maltreated.

Q.—What made them maltreat you?

Thukoree.—To get money from us.

Q.—Then those who paid were of course well treated and released?

Thukoree.—Not so; those who could not pay were beaten in hopes that their friends would in time pay; and those who paid, were beaten in hopes that their friends would be made in time to pay more.

Q.—I understand that some forty Thugs died from the beating, and confinement?

Thukoree.—No; not from the beatings; forty or more died, but they were all killed by a great

* All that is here stated is strictly true.

demon that every night visited our prison and killed or tortured some one.

All.—Yes; that demon is well remembered to this day, we have all heard him a hundred times described by the survivors.

Thukoree.—I saw him only once myself. I was awake while all the rest were asleep; he came in at the door, and seemed to swell as he came in till his head touched the roof, and the roof was very high, and his bulk became enormous. I prostrated myself, and told him that " he was our Purmesur, " (Great God) and we poor helpless mortals depend- " ing entirely upon his will." This pleased him, and he passed by me; but took such a grasp at the man Mungulee, who slept by my side, that he was seized with spasms all over from the nape of the neck to the sole of his foot.

Q.—Was this the way they all died?

Thukoree.—Yes; this was his mode of annoying them, and but few survived. They all died like Mungulee. They had rheumatic pains and spasms all over, and the prison was for a long time visited by him every night.

Q.—Was it in the cold and rainy season?

Thukoree.—We were in more than a whole year, but this spirit came most often in the cold and rainy weather.

Q.—Who seized you?

Thukoree.—We were seized by Komere and Puhar, *Kuckwahas,* and Durcear the *Rathore,* Zumeendars.

Feringeea.—Yes; and not a soul of their families are now left to pour the libation at their funeral obsequies!

Thukoree.—Yes; they were severely punished afterwards for giving us so much annoyance.

Q.—By whom ?
Thukoree.—By *Davey.*
Q.—How many were you ?
Thukoree.—We were one hundred and thirty-three seized, at the requisition of the Mynporee magistrate, who might have had the whole if he liked, but he wanted only four, and four were sent to him ; but the only evidence against them was Aman, the father of Birjee, who died here in jail after the Lucknadown murders, and he became so much frightened that he let the cup of Ganges water fall out of his hands before the magistrate, who did not in consequence believe him ; and they were all four released, though they were all present at the murder of Lieutenant Monsell. One was Ruttee Ram, who was hung at Indore 1829, and for whom you paid a thousand rupees ; Bukut hung at Saugor 1832 ; Deena, the father of Munohur, approver, and Hurnam a Zumeendar of Murnae. 129 were kept in confinement, and for each of these men 129 rupees were taken. They got above sixteen thousand rupees. Fourteen thousand of them were paid to the Subah of Nodha Rae Sing, Havildar. The very day that the money was paid into his treasury, his son and a fine horse of his died, and he was himself taken ill. He was summoned to Gwalior, and when he offered the money to Doulut Rae Scindheea, the Bala Bae, the daughter of Madhajee Scindheea, whom he used to consult on all public affairs, told him that her father owed his death to the execution of some of these strange people at Muthura ; and that he had better not meddle with the money that Rae Sing had so foolishly extorted from them ; that it was money acquired by murder, and that those who got it seemed to be under some supernatural influence.

Doulut Rae told Rae Sing to give away all the money in charity, and release the survivors. He did so, but it was too late ; his sickness and misery continued and · he died. Doulut Rae was the adopted son of Madhajee Scindheea ; Bala Bae was his real daughter, and a very wise and good woman.

Q.—What made you all go to Nodha ?

Thukoree.—Mr. Halhed attacked our villages, and after Lieutenant Monsell had been killed, we did not think ourselves any longer safe. Aman Sing, called the Raw Sahib, was the chief of Nodha, and he would have protected us, as there had been a compact between us and his family ; but he had been removed, and Rae Sing sent us the Amil.

Q.—What were the villages you occupied in Sindouse, and Murnae ?

Thukoree.—We occupied sixteen out of the fifty-two villages of Sursaedhar, and the sixteen villages of Sindouse, most of which we formed and peopled. All these villages are situated in the Delta of the Sinde and the Koharee rivers, near where they· join and flow together into the Jumna.

Q.—Whence did you come to occupy these villages ?

Thukoree.—The Bursotes and some other of the original Mahommadan clans, after trying to establish themselves at Agra, came to Akoopore in the Dooab, and were protected in their vocations for forty years by the Gour Rajah ; but he demanding too great a share of the booty, they left his country, and came to Himmutpore on the bank of Jumna, and took up their abode under the protection of the Sengur Raja Juggummum Sa, from whom the fort and town of Juggummunpore derive their name.* He became in time too exorbitant in his demands for a share of the booty, and family after family left his territory, and established themselves in the Purheear, on Sindouse purguna—some occupying old, and some forming new villages, and in time they constituted the entire population of the greater part, cultivating all the lands - themselves, and extending their expeditions annually into distant countries. At all these different seats the old clans made new converts from all casts of Hindoos, Brahmuns, Rajpoots, cowherds, shepherds, and others.

Feringeea.—My ancestors were not among the people who came this way to Sindouse. The fort of Sursae was held by Rajahs of the Meoo cast, whence the term Mewatee. The Brahmuns of the village of Tehngoor served them as household priests; and when one of these Meeo Rajahs went to wait upon the Emperor at Delhi, some of these Brahmuns accompanied him, and there they were initiated in the mysteries of Thuggee; and on their return they introduced it among their friends at Murnae and other places in the Sursae or Omuree purguna. Our great progenitors Seeam and Asa went to Murnae to seek employment about seven generations ago, and were there married into the Tehngoorea families, and became initiated in the mysteries of Thuggee, and from that time it has descended without interruption in the family. Every male as he became of age, became a Thug.

Q.—Is this true Kharndee?

---

* From Juggummun Sa there have been, it is said, Pem or Pertab Sa his son, Somere Sa, son of Pem Sa, Rutun Sa, son of Somere Sa, Rukut, son of Rutun, and Muhepat Sa, son of Rukut— the present Rajah, who holds his estate under the Rajah of Jhalone.

Kharndee and *Nundun.*—This has been believed ever since we can remember, and the Kusbatee and Porasur Brahmuns in the same way married into Tehngoorea and Kunouj families, and became Thugs like themselves.

Thukoree.—The Tehngooreas and Kunouj Brahmans did not certainly come with the emigrants from Agra. They were in Sursae long before, but how they got there I know not.

Feringeea.—There was a Rajah of Kuchwaha who has since become a god. His image is still worshipped in our village of Murnae. He was the Rajah of Lahae, and had three sons, Ruttun Sing, Anoord Sing, and Mehngoo. Mehngoo came to Roragow, one of the fifty-two villages of Sursae, and having invited all the Meeo chiefs to a feast he got them all put to death, and established himself as Rajah, and from that time it became a Kuchwaha Rajpoot Raj. The Tehngoor Brahmuns served them as they had served the Meeo Rajahs as household priests. Rutun Sing reigned over Lalae, Mehngoo over Sursae, and the third brother over Amaen.

Q.—How came the tax of 24 rupees 8 anas to be first imposed upon you?

Thukoree.—Thugs had always been obliged to make occasional presents to the chiefs and heads of villages under whose protection they resided, but there was never any fixed rate of payment. The handsomest horse, sword or ornament, that they got in an expedition was commonly reserved for the most powerful patron of the order. At last two of the ancestors of Feringeea, Hirroulee and Rae Sing in an expedition to the south across the Nurbudda river got a booty worth some hundred and forty thousand rupees. Rae Sing had secreted one of the diamonds which weighed a rupee, and in the division of the spoil on their return home a quarrel ensued. In his rage Rae Sing said to Hirroulee, " that a man who could not keep his " mother from the embraces of a tanner of hides " might be contented with what others chose to " give him." Hirroulee had no arms on, but calling upon his friend Telokee Rajpoot for vengeance, he stabbed Rae Sing in the belly with his spear. His bowels burst out, but we got a silver plate applied to the wound and Rae Sing recovered ; but was for a long time obliged to wear the silver plate. Rae Sing went to the Rana of Gohud, from whom he got the farm of the customs for one hundred and thirty thousand rupees a year, and the farm of the purguna of Omree or Sursae at sixty thousand. He induced the chief of Gohud to invade Sindouse, which was burned to the ground, and from that time the Thug families were made to pay every three years a tax of twenty-five rupees each. Rae Sing sold the large diamond afterwards for sixty-five thousand rupees ; and the rest of the booty was estimated at sixty-seven thousand.

Hirroulee went off to the Rajah of Rampoora, Kuleean Sing, and gave him a present of four thousand rupees to espouse his quarrel. He got in return the village of Koorcha, granted in rent-free tenure, and built there a fine well that still goes by his name.

Q.—And had Hirroulee's mother gone off with the Chumar ?

Feringeea.—It is too true ; she went off with the Chumar, and that crime has accelerated the ruin of our family.

Q.—When were the Sonars murdered at Murnae ?

Dorgha.—When Rae Sing and Hirroulee brought home the great booty, they sent Dorgha and another Sonar as usual to fetch merchants from Oude to buy it. They came with two merchants and bought a good deal, but Hirroulee's wife wanted to see how we killed people as she had heard a good deal about it, and they were all four strangled for her entertainment I have. heard.

Lalmun.—Not so; I was present on that occasion; Hirroulee had been dead some time, when the Sonars and two merchants came to buy some of her jewels, which Hirroulee had secreted. They said they had ready money in order to tempt her to sell them cheap, and the widow persuaded some of her friends to kill them. They were strangled and buried, but instead of seven thousand rupees, which the widow expected, we got only seven hundred. The families of the Sonars made a great noise when they could not be found. Kulecan Sing Rajah, of Rampoora, came, and found the bodies, plundered the widow and turned her out naked, and levied a fine from all, saying that now we had begun to murder at home as well as abroad, we were no longer deserving of favour.

Inaent.—I saw the widow afterwards begging her way through Saugor, and she died of starvation at Sehwas in Bhopaul.

Thukoree.—When Sursae and Sindouse came under Gwalior, the Gwalior amil continued to levy the tax upon the Thugs through Láljoo Choudhuree the Zumeendar. He divided them all into families, and each family was rated at twenty-four rupees eight anas every three years, upon which he as collector, got a per centage. But in his accounts rendered to the amil he inserted, as one family under the ostensible head, many branches who had separated and from whom he levied the tax separately. He therefore collected a great deal more than he accounted for. Laljoo after the murder of Lieut. Monsell, was imprisoned in the Bareilly jail, and was succeeded in the Zumeendaree of Sindouse by his son Suntokerae. The purguna of Sindouse came under the Company's government, but that of Sursea continued under Gwalior.

Sheikh Inaent.—After the attack of Mr. Halhed we thought that part of the country very unsafe, and a great many come off to Bundlecund, and the Bhopaul and Nurbudda districts.

PRESENT INAENT, DIBBA, MIHRBAN, BHEEKUN KHAN AND OTHERS.

Q.—Tell me all you recollect about the expedition in which you were seized, Inaent?

Sheikh Inaent.—After the Duschra of 1829, several gangs united from different points at the village of Kohpa, between Jubulpore and Banda, about forty from the districts of Futtehgur and Cawnpore under Rambuksh, Mihrban and others, twelve under Bhola Buneea from Jhalone, and twenty-five under myself from Jhansee. We intended to operate that season upon the great road from Mirzapore to Jubulpore, and strike off to that between Saugor and Calpee when necessary. We came on to Shahnagur, and there leaving the main body I came on with Rambuksh, Bhola, and fifteen other Thugs to the village of Pureyna to search for *Bunij.* Here we met two shop-keepers, two blacksmiths and a Musulman trooper, on their way from the Duekun to the Dooab; and having won their confidence in the usual manner we sent them on to our friends with four of our party, and a message to say that they would find them worth taking; at night we rejoined the main body and found Dibba Jemadar entertaining the travellers. We set out the next morning intending to put them to death on the road to Biseynee, but we found so many parties of Brinjaras encamped and moving along that road that we could not manage it. The next morning we went on with them from Biseynee, and at a nalah in the jungle three cose distant we killed them at about eight o'clock in the morning. The bodies were buried under some stones where your people afterwards found them. We returned through Biseynee to Shahnagur, and thence came in upon the great road to Mirzaporee at the village of Sewagunge. In the evening four travellers came up on their way from Jubulpore to Banda, and were persuaded to pass the night with us on the bank of the tank. We were preparing to go on with them after the third watch with the intention of killing them on the road, when we heard the *Duheea* (the call or cry of the hare) a dreadful omen, and we let them go on unmolested.

Soon after four Sipahees of the 73d regiment, came up and sat down at the fire to warm themselves. The regiment was on its march from Jubulpore to Banda, and the four Sipahees were a little in advance of it. After some conversation they went on, and we prepared to set out, having thrown into the fire some clothes and a churee (a painted stick as a badge of office) belonging to the trooper whom we had murdered. While we were preparing, the two men whom you had sent on with the regiment, Dhun Sing and Doulut, came

up and sat down to warm themselves.* We over-
heard Doulut say to Dhun Sing " this stick and these
clothes must have belonged to murdered men, and
these must be some of our old friends, and a large
party of them," and both seemed to be alarmed at
their situation as they were then alone. I made a
point of being the last off, and my brother Sheikh
Chund, who was lately hung, had already mounted
his horse, and I had my foot in the stirrup when
they saw part of the advanced guard and immediately made a rush at our bridles. We drew our
swords but it was too late. Chand Khan jumped
off his horse and made off, both fell upon me, and I
was secured. Had Doulut and Dhun Sing called
out Thugs, the guard might have secured a great
part of the gang, but they appeared to be panic
struck, and unable to speak. By this time the
regiment came up, and finding some of the remains
of the troopers' clothes on the fire, the European
officers found it difficult to prevent the Sipahees
from bayonetting me on the spot. I put on a bold
face, and told them that they ought all to be ashamed
of themselves to allow a native gentleman to be
thus insulted and maltreated on the high road, and
that nothing but the dread of the same ruffianly
treatment had made my friends run off and leave
me. I had three brothers in that gang ; they were
all afterwards taken ; two have been hung and the
third is here.

---

* Dhun Sing and Doulut were two approvers whom I got from
Mr. Maddock at Sehore in 1828, and sent off with Lieut. James
Sleeman, of the 73d, on his march from Jubulpore to Banda with
his regiment, in the hope of meeting with these gangs on the great
roads to Mirzapore. I was then in the civil charge of the district
of Jubulpore.—W. H. S.

Q.—What did you do after Sheikh had been taken?

Bheekun Khan.—We Musulmans of his gang took the road to Biseynee through Belehree; the Dooab men went off on the road to Mirzapore, and Bhola and his party went to their homes. While we were resting at a village two cose on the other side of Beleheree, in this district, two carriers of Ganges water, two tailors and a woman came up on their way to Banda, and having rested and taken some refreshments with us, they went on in our company to Shahnagur, where we passed the night, and the next day we went on together to Biseynee, where we fell in with two other travellers on their way to Banda. These two men we found so poor that we tried to get rid of them, as they might be some obstacle to our designs upon the five, and could yield us nothing. We tried to get off without waking them, but in vain ; they got up and we tried to persuade them that it was too soon for them to set out, but in vain. We then sent four of our party with orders to take them along the high road while we struck off on the bye path by which we usually took our victims on that road. They soon after got alarmed, and insisted upon being taken to the main body which they had seen strike off to the right. The four Thugs were obliged to consent, and they soon overtook us. It was now determined that they also should die, and six of our party were desired to attend them and move on a little faster than the main body to the nalah in the jungle, where we usually killed people. We slackened our pace, and as soon as the six men reached the nalah they put the two men to death, and concealed their bodies till we came up, when the other five persons were strangled; and the bodies of all seven were buried under the stones near the place where we had buried the five men whom we killed in our advance, and where we the next year killed the five Byragees and the Sipahee. All these eighteen bodies I pointed out to Chundee-deen, Subahdar of the 4th regiment, whom you sent with me from Saugor in 1832.* From the two poor men we got only one rupee; but from the others we got two hundred; and in the division Chand Khan and Dulole, who have been hung at Saugor, took the share of their brother Seikh Inaent who had been arrested by the 73d regiment.

Q.—Is this true?

Sheikh Inaent.—I believe so; they gave my share to my wife.

Q.—And what did you Dooab Thugs do in your flight?

Dibba.—We did not rest till we had got thirty miles in advance of the regiment on the Mirzapore road. We then halted and spent the night at a small village, and were going on again the next morning when we fell in with four Gosaens, a Brahmun and a Rajpoot, on their way from Hydrabad to Mirzapore. They went on with us to Omurpatun in Rewa, whence we set out with them before daylight, and on reaching the place that had been chosen the evening before they were all six strangled. It was about an hour before daylight. After we had examined the booty and made the grave, we went to take up the bodies, but one of the six got up and tried to run away. He had got off about a hundred yards when he was overtaken and strangled again.

Q.—Did he not call out?

* These bodies were all taken up by the party under the Subahdar,

Miherban.—Yes; but he had been so much hurt in the neck the first time that he could not be heard at any distance; and we had no sooner brought his body back and put it down among the others, than we heard the servants of Captain Nicolson coming up.* The Captain was coming from Mirzapore, and was to encamp that day at Omurpatum. As soon as we heard his servants coming up we all made off, leaving the bodies unburied; a white pony belonging to Esuree Jemadar got loose and ran towards the servants, who called out to know whose it was; and thinking they must come up before we could dispose of the bodies we made off and left the pony behind us. Whether they discovered the bodies or not I do not know; but the people of the town must have seen them.

Q.—Had the man been able to raise his voice, the servants must, you think, have heard him?

Miherban.—Certainly. They were within hearing at the time.

Q.—Who strangled the man who attempted to run off?

Miherban.—Dibba and two of his men went after him, and strangled him.

Dibba.—That is not true. Persaud, who is now with Mr. Wilson, and Dojja, who is still at large, cut him down with their swords. We did not strangle him.

Q.—Did not part of your gangs after the arrest of Sheikh Inaent proceed and join that of Feringeea between Saugor and Bhopaul?

Zolfukar.—When Inaent was seized I was with a gang of twenty-four Thugs at Shahnugur coming

* Captain and Mrs. Nicolson came that morning to Omurpatam, on their way from Mizarpore to Jubulpore.

up with the others. Mahumud Büksh was with
another of seven at Biseynee. Bhola Buneea in
his flight came up and told us of Inaent's arrest.
We went as fast as we could through Saugor
towards Bhopaul, and at Sehora we fell in with
Feringeea coming from Bhopaul with a gang of
forty Thugs. He returned with us and we proceeded to Bhopaul without killing any person.
From Bhopaul we retraced our steps towards
Saugor, and at Omaree fell in with the Farsee and
his servant and two Buneeas whom we killed. But
before we killed them we had fallen in with a gang
of eighteen Lodhies from the Dooab, and having
shared in the booty, they left us to operate upon
the Seronge roads. We had also fallen in with
Noor Khan Jemadar and his gang of seven men,
and they also shared in the booty of the Farsee.

After the Lodhies left us, we came on to Bhilsa
where we fell in with three men and two women,
whom we killed near Manora, Ramdeen Sipahee
of Bhopaul and his mother on their way home to
Banda, a bearer, his wife and brother. Coming on
to Baghrode we fell in with two men who told us
that three of their companions had been plundered
by robbers, and were behind. We came on to
Bahadurpore with them, and killed them between
that place and the village of Mirzapore. We had
left people to detain the three who were coming
up as we thought they could have nothing left after
the robbery. They asked after their two companions, and we told them that they were pushing on
as fast as they could for Saugor.

We now struck off upon the Hoshungabad road,
and at Belehra met Mahamud Buksh's gang of
seven Thugs, and went on to Raneepore, where we
killed two men, and another at Kurheya Khera.

Here to our great surprise and consternation, my mare dropped a foal, and we all came under the Eetuk, all contaminated alike; we separated to return home. I with a party of about thirty came through Bishunkera, Bhopaul, Bhilsa and Saugor home.

Mahamud Buksh.—Near Bagrode three bearers and a Bhistee came up while we were washing ourselves in the stream, on their way from Bhopaul to Saugor, and told us, in the course of conversation, that they had seen your guard seize a number of people very like us near Bhilsa. We knew it must be Feringeea's party, and fearing that these men would get us also seized on the road, we killed them and got home all safe.

Feringeea.—We were bathing at a river four cose this side of Bhilsa when I heard directly over my head the *Chireya.** I was much alarmed, and Kurhora, who is an excellent augur, told me that I ought to take the gang back on the Gunj Basoda road immediately after so bad an omen;' but I determined upon coming on towards Saugor two cose to the village of Murue. On reaching this place I tied my horse to a tree, and went into the village to talk with the Putel, leaving the gang near the horse. While talking with him I heard a great uproar and saw my horse running towards the village, and on going to catch him, saw your Nujeebs seizing and binding my gang. There were forty, but they secured only twenty-eight. I made off as I was half dressed and get home, and twelve of my gang escaped. Had I attended to Kurhora's advice you would have had none of us, another proof of the efficacy of omens if attended to. My

* See Vocabulary,—*Chireya.*

adopted son Hurreea, and Mahadeo pointed out
the bodies of most of the people whom we murdered in that expedition; the rest were taken up
by Zolfukar himself last year.

Mahamud Buksh.—It was a very unfortunate
expedition. At Biseynee we fell in with some travellers, and should have secured them, but when
Zolfukar came up, Bhola, who is always talking,
could not help saying in *Ramasee*—" After all we
" shall not go home without something to please
" our wives and children." The travellers heard,
suspected our designs, left our encampment on the
bank of the tank, and went into the village. This
was our first banij (merchandize) and to lose it
thus was a bad omen: it was in fact like being
seized. Then came the murder of the women at
Manora, and to crown the whole, *the fouling of
Zolfukar's mare which brought us all under the
Eetuk.* Every think seemed to go wrong with us
that season, and I often proposed to return home
and open the expedition anew, but I was unhappily
over-ruled.

Q.—How did the guard of Nujeebs pass without
seeing you?

Mahamud Buksh.—We have never been able to
understand. We came the direct road to Saugor
and they passed us on that road in advancing to
Bhilsa. We never saw them, nor did they see us.

Q.—How did you afterwards allow yourself to
be taken?

Feringeea.—Having lived among the clans of
Rajpootana and Telingana for years together, I
should have gone off to some of them, but you had
secured my mother, wife and child. I could not
forsake them—was always inquiring after them,
and affording my pursuers the means of tracing

me. I knew not what indignities my wife and mother might suffer. Could I have felt secure that they would suffer none, I should not have been taken.

Q.—You were in General Ochterlony's service for some time. How did that happen?

Feringcea.—My cousin, Aman Sing Subadar, after the death of his brother, Dureear, and my father, Purusram, became our guardian. His mother was one of the first families in the country, and her sister's son, Jhundee alias Gunga Sing, had the command of two regiments at Kotah. Having no sons of his own, he asked Aman to give him either me or Phoolsa, the son of Dureear, for whom you have offered two hundred rupees, for adoption, as he had great wealth and no child to leave it to. He suspected Aman to be a thief, but knew not that he was a leader of assassins, or he would have had nothing to say to us.

Q.—But did not Aman's mother know that he was so?

Feringcea.—Not till long after she was married, and from that time she was never suffered to visit her sister. Phoolsa would not consent to live with Gunga Sing Kuptan, nor should I, had I not had a dispute with Aman while out on a Thug expedition. I went to him, and he became very fond of me, and got me made a Subahdar in the grenadier company of the Buldeo regiment. I could not live without some of my old Thug friends, and got Rambuksh my cousin, for whom you have offered five hundred rupees, enlisted and made a Havildar on my own security for his good conduct. He was always a very loose character, and when Gunga Sing went to Oudeepore with his two regiments as the body guard of the young Queen, who was the daughter of the Kotah Chief, Rambuksh seduced a young widow, the daughter of one of the most respectable bankers of the city, who became pregnant. As soon as the intrigue was discovered, she pounded and ate the diamond of her own ring, or something of the kind, and died, and Rambuksh was obliged to fly to save his life, which was demanded by her family of the chief. Having given security for his good conduct, I thought my own head in danger, and fled to Boondee, where I contrived to get into the service of Major Tod, recommended to him by the post master as a young man of high birth and great promise. On going to meet General Ochterlony at Bheelwara soon after, he recommended me to him, and he made me Jemadar of Hurcaras. I attended him to Delhi and to Ajmere, whence he sent me in charge of the post office peons to Rewaree. From this place I was sent with four peons to attend a young lady of the General's family from Delhi to Calcutta. Her escort consisted of a Havildar, a Naek, and twenty Sipahees, under the command of Bhowanee Sing, Jemadar of the local regiment. We reached Muthura without any accident, and lodged in Colonel Gunge. At night Bhowanee Sing was caught in an awkward position with one of the young lady's women, and dreading the vengeance of the general, he and all his guard fled. He roused me, told me what had happened, and advised me to go off with him and try our fortunes with Runjeet Sing. This I declined; but hearing that my cousin Aman Subahdar had gone that season with his gang into Rajpootana, I started, and passing through Hindone and Beeana, joined them at Kuraulee, after having been absent from him some years. It was, I believe the year after I rejoined Aman that my

gang was arrested at Kotah, and that we killed
Ashraf Khan, the Subahdar Major of the 4th
cavalry and his party. From that time till I was
taken, or about ten years, I was always out with
my gang except in the season of the rains; and for
several even of these seasons we were out in Rajpootana, where the rains offer little impediment.
Indeed in the western parts of Rajpootana Thugs
have an advantage in the rainy season, as at the
other seasons the most wealthy travellers move
along in wheeled carriages, and cannot be so easily
managed as on foot or on horseback, to which
mode of travelling they are obliged to have recourse
in the rains.

Q.—Is Gunga Sing still living?

Feringeea.—No, I have just heard from Jowahir,
one of the Thugs whom Lieutenant Briggs has sent
in, that he died four years ago at Oudeepore.

Q.—Did your wife know that you were a Thug?

Feringeea.—Neither she nor her family knew it
till you seized her and had her brought to Jubulpore, where she found poor Jhurhoo and the other
members of my gang taken at Bhilsa. Her family
are of the aristocracy of Jhansee and Sumtur, as
you may know.

Q.—Do not the Brinjaras often perpetrate murder
in their encampments?

Feringeea.—Just before the twenty-six of my
gang were taken by you at Bhilsa, and before Zolfukar joined us, we were cooking our dinner in the
afternoon at a village three cose this side of Sehore,
when five travellers came up on their way to Bhilsa.
We tried to prevail upon them to wait for us, but
they went on, saying they should spend the night
at Hirora, a village four cose further on. We
made sure of securing them at Hirora, and remained

19*

where we were to dine. We reached Hirora
about nine at night, and searched all the village in
vain for the travellers. We knew that they must
either have suspected our designs, or been disposed
of by other Thugs on the road; and I recollected
that about three miles from Hirora we had passed
a Brinjara encampment. In the morning I went
back with a few followers, and there found a horse
and a pony that we had seen with the five travellers.
" What have you done with the five travellers, my
" good friends. You have taken from us our mer-
" chandise ?" " Bunij," said I in Rumasee. They
apologized for what they had done ; said they did
not know we were after them, and offered to share
the booty with us; but I said we had no fair claim
to a share, since none of our party were present at
the *loading*—(killing). We left them and came on
to Bhilsa where we met your party of Nujeebs.

Q.—And these Brinjaree Thugs are rarely seized
or punished ?

Sahih Khan, of Telingana.—How can their
deeds be known. They do all their work themselves. They live in the desert and work in the
desert. We live in villages, and cannot do our
work without the convenience and support of the
farmers who hold, and the influential men who
occupy them. Local authorities of all kinds and
degrees must be conciliated by us ; but these men
are relieved from all this cost and trouble by foregoing the pleasure of other men's society, and the
comforts of a fixed habitation. They are wiser
men than we are !

Morlee.—I was one day walking with some of
our party near Jeypore by an encampment of
wealthy merchants from the westward, who wore
very high turbans. I observed to my friends as

we passed "what enormous turbans these men wear!" using our mystick term *Aghasee.* The most respectable among them came up immediately and invited us to sit down with them, saying, " my " good friends, we are of your fraternity, though " our *Aghasees* are not the same." They told us that they were now opulent merchants, and independent of Thuggee, the trade by which they had chiefly acquired their wealth ; but that they still did a little occasionally when they found in a suitable place a Bunij worth taking; but that they were now beyond speculating in trifles! We were kindly entertained, and much pleased with our new friends, but left them the same day, and I have never met any men of the kind since. The common Moltanee Thugs, who strangle men with the thongs which they use in driving their bullocks, we have often met. They are to be found all over India, but abound most to the north-west.

Q.—What—among the Sieks?

Morlee.—Yes ; but they are not themselves Sieks. They are what we call Moltanee Thugs chiefly.

Q.—Have you ever known a Siek Thug?

Morlee.—Never. I never saw a Siek take to Thuggee.

Sahib Khan.—I know Ram Sing Siek : he was a noted Thug leader; a very shrewd man. He resided and still resides at Borhanpore, and used to act with Ram Sing (who was hung here at Jubulpore last month) and Rama Dheemur, and Mohun Sing, son of Pahar Sing of Poona. He served with the celebrated Sheikh Dulloo as a Pindaree for some years after he had become distinguished as a Thug, but returned to Thuggee, and acted with his old associates for two years about Borhampore, when he went off again and joined Sheikh Dulloo. He sold

Dulloo a very fine horse, for which he could never get payment; and as he wanted money he got annoyed. A large reward had then been offered by the Company for Dulloo's head. He left him for a month or two, and on coming back, Dulloo who was annoyed at his importunity, instead of advancing to embrace him as usual, merely got up from his charpae (couch) and put one foot upon the floor keeping the other upon the couch. That slight decided his fate. Ram Sing had been long thinking of the reward, and he now determined to win it. He killed Sheikh Dulloo either that night or the night following, and took his head to Colonel Seyer at Elichpore. The colonel said that he was sorry so brave a man should have been-killed in so cowardly a manner, and sent Ram Sing to get his reward from Dhunraj Seth at Omrowtee. Dhunraj knew that Ram Sing was the Thug who had murdered a party of his treasure bearers. He arrested him, and soon after got hold of his friends Pahar Sing, his son Mohun Sing, and Rama Dheemur. They soon after made their escape from prison, and Ram Sing is now at his old trade in Berhampore. He never either got paid for his horse, or for the murder of Sheikh Dulloo.*

Q.—How often had you been on Thuggee before you saw a murder?

Sheikh Inaent.—It was on my return from the

---

* *Extract of a Letter from Lieutenant Graham, Assistant Magistrate in Khandeish, to the address of Captain W. H. Sleeman, dated the 5th November, 1835.*

"Of the other Thugs mentioned as residing about Borhampore, Ram Sing died at Dhoobo, four years ago; he was the person who murdered the famous Pindarra Chief Shaikh Dullah, on whose head a reward of 15,000 rupees was placed."

(True Extract)
W. H. SLEEMAN, *General Superintendent.*

first expedition which I made with my father to the Duckun, when I was fifteen years of age, and about thirty-five years ago. We were a gang of about eighty or ninety Thugs under my father Hinga and some of the Duckun chiefs, lodged in the Maasoleum outside of the town of Elichpore. Two of our leaders, Gumboo and Laljoo, on going into the Bazar fell in with the grooms of the Nawab Subjee Khan, the uncle of the Nawab of Bhopaul Wuzeer Muhommud Khan, who told them that their master had been with his son and his two hundred horse in the service of the Nizam at Hydrabad; and having had a quarrel with his son he was now on his way home to Bhopaul. They came back and reported; and Dulele Khan and Khuleel Khan and other leaders of fame went and introduced themselves to the Nawab, pretending that they had been to the Duckun with horses for sale, and were now on their way back to Hindostan. He was pleased with their address and appearance, and invited them to return the next day, which they did; and the following day he set out with as many of our gang as it was thought safe to exhibit. He had two grooms, two troopers, and a slave girl, two horses and a mare with a wound in the neck, and a pony. The slave girl's duty was to prepare for him his daily portion of subzee, and he told us that he had got the name of Subzee Khan from the quantity of that drug which he was accustomed to drink.

We came on together three stages, and during the fourth stage we came to an extensive jungle this side of Dhoba, and in the Baitool district; and on reaching a nalah about nine o'clock Khuleel said, " Khan Sahib, we have had a fatiguing jour- " ney, and we had better rest here, and take some "refreshment." "By all means," said the Nawab, "I feel a little fatigued and will take my Subzee "here." He dismounted, laid his sword and shield upon the ground, spread his carpet and sat down. Dulcle and Khuleel sat down by his side while the girl was preparing his potion, of which he invited these two men, as our supposed chiefs, to partake ; and the grooms were engaged with the horses, and the troopers were smoking their pipes at a distance. It had been determined that the Nawab should be first secured, for he was a powerful man, and if he had a moment's warning he would certainly have cut down some of the gang before they could secure him. Laljoo also went and sat near him, while Gomanee stood behind and seemed to be much interested in the conversation. All being now ready the signal was given, and the Nawab was strangled by Gomanee, while Laljoo and Dulele held his legs. As soon as the others saw the Nawab secured they fell upon his attendants, and all were strangled, and their bodies were buried in the bed of the water course. On going back to Elichpore, Gomanee sold the Nawab's shield for eight rupees, but it was worth so much more that the people suspected him, and came to our camp to search for him. Our spies brought us timely notice and we concealed him under the housings of our horses.

Q.—What was the cause of the quarrel between him and his son?

Inaent.—The son in a passion had drawn his sword and cut the Nawab's favourite mare over the neck. A quarrel ensued, and he left his son in charge of the squadron of horse to return to Bhopaul.*

Q.—And this was the first murder you ever witnessed?

Inaent.—This was the first, and it made a great impression upon my mind, and you may rely upon the correctness of what I state regarding it.

* Reference having been made to the Court of Bhopaul through the Political Agent; this story is found to be quite true.

END OF VOLUME I.